STEAL THIS FLASH PRESENTS

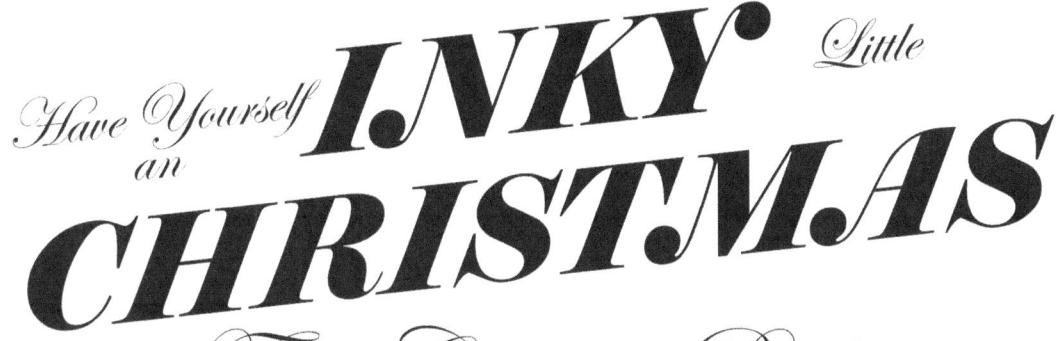

Have Yourself an **INKY** *Little* **CHRISTMAS** *Tattoo Coloring Book*

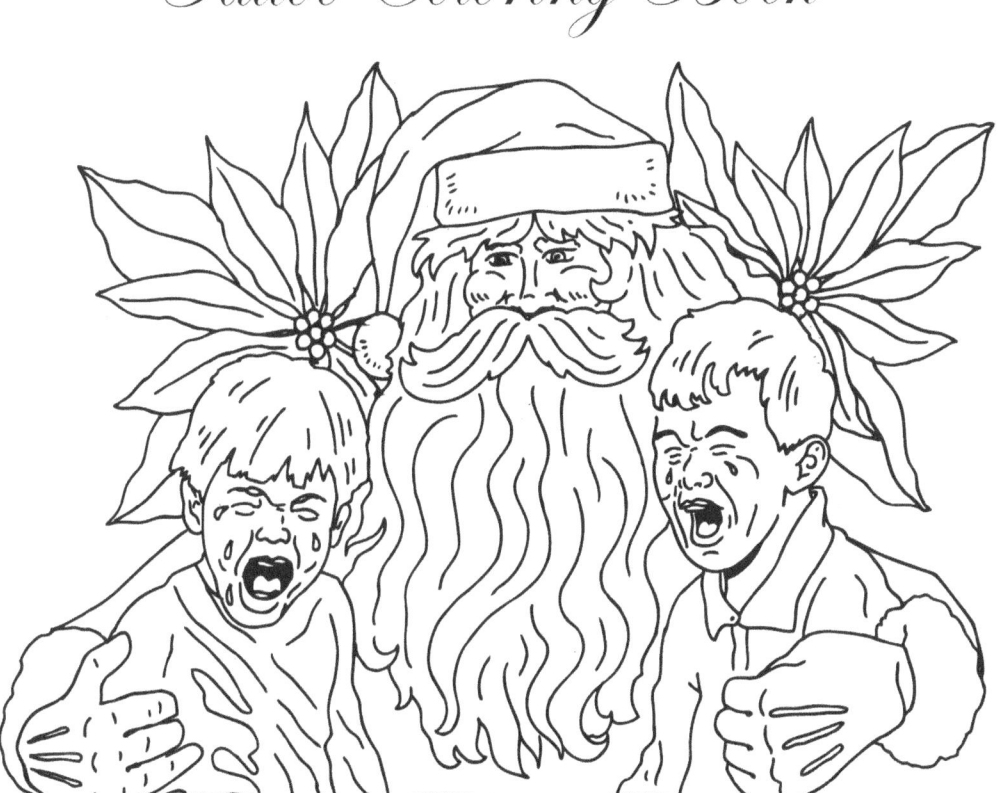

©2020 CJ HUGHES FOR STEAL THIS FLASH.

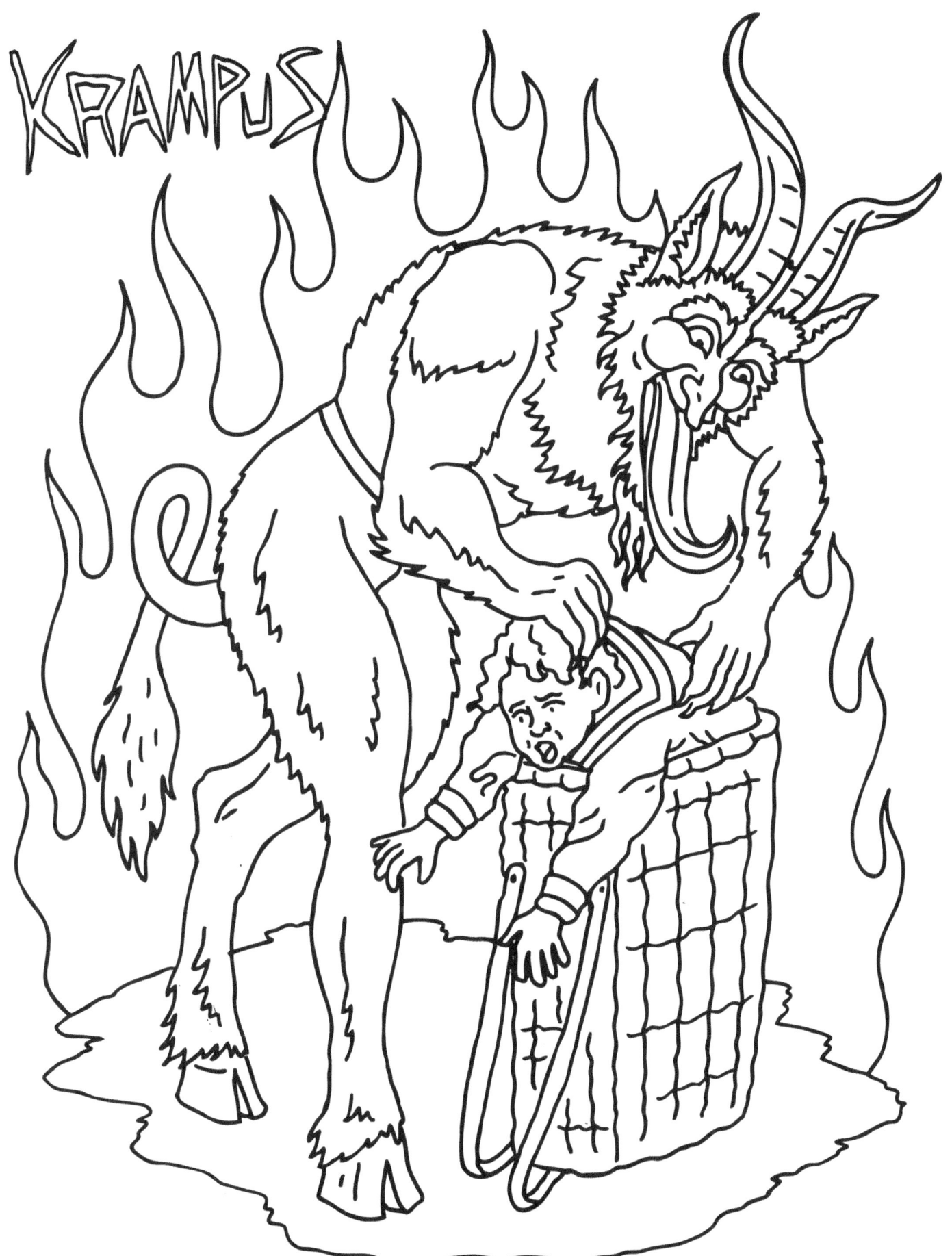

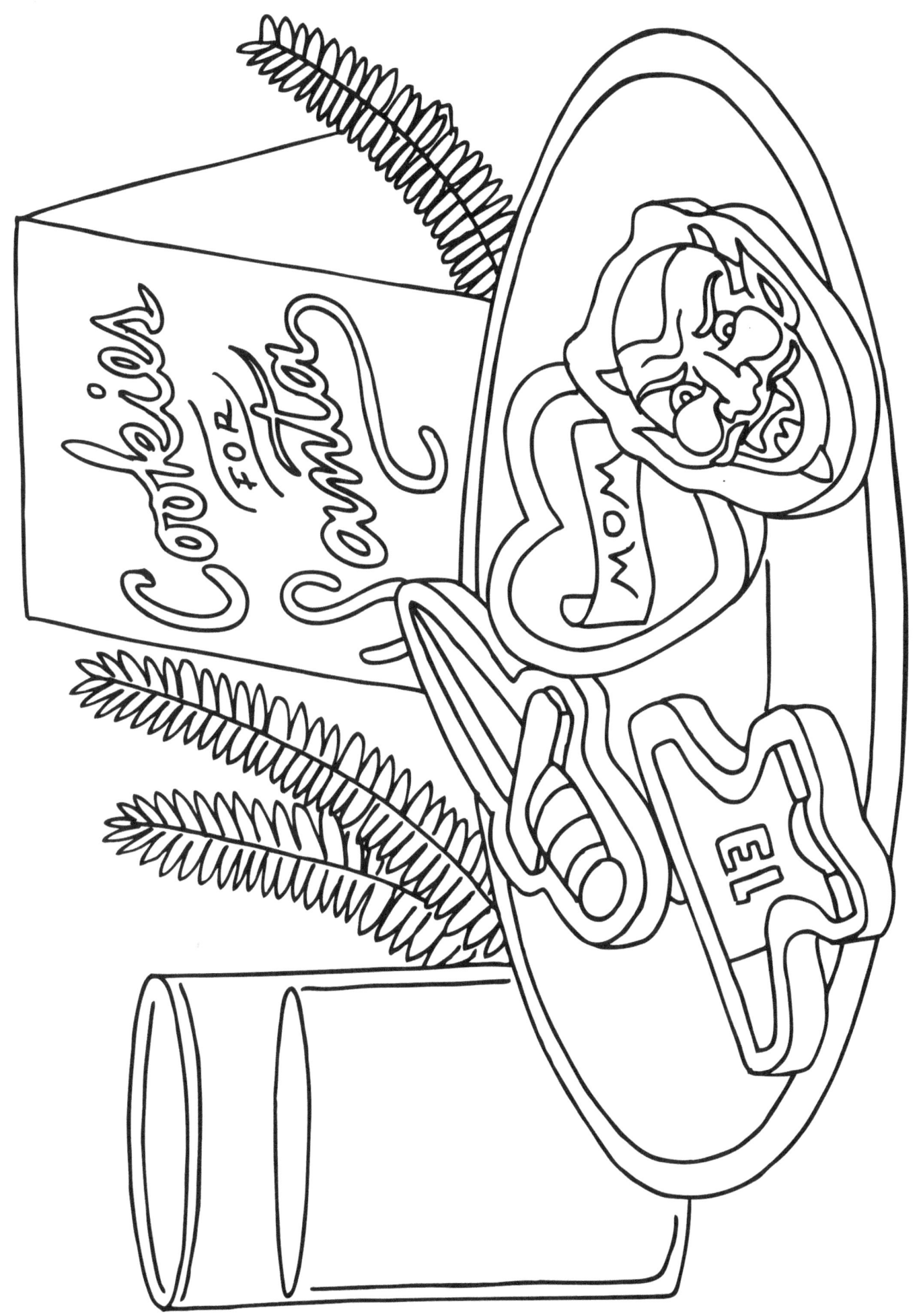

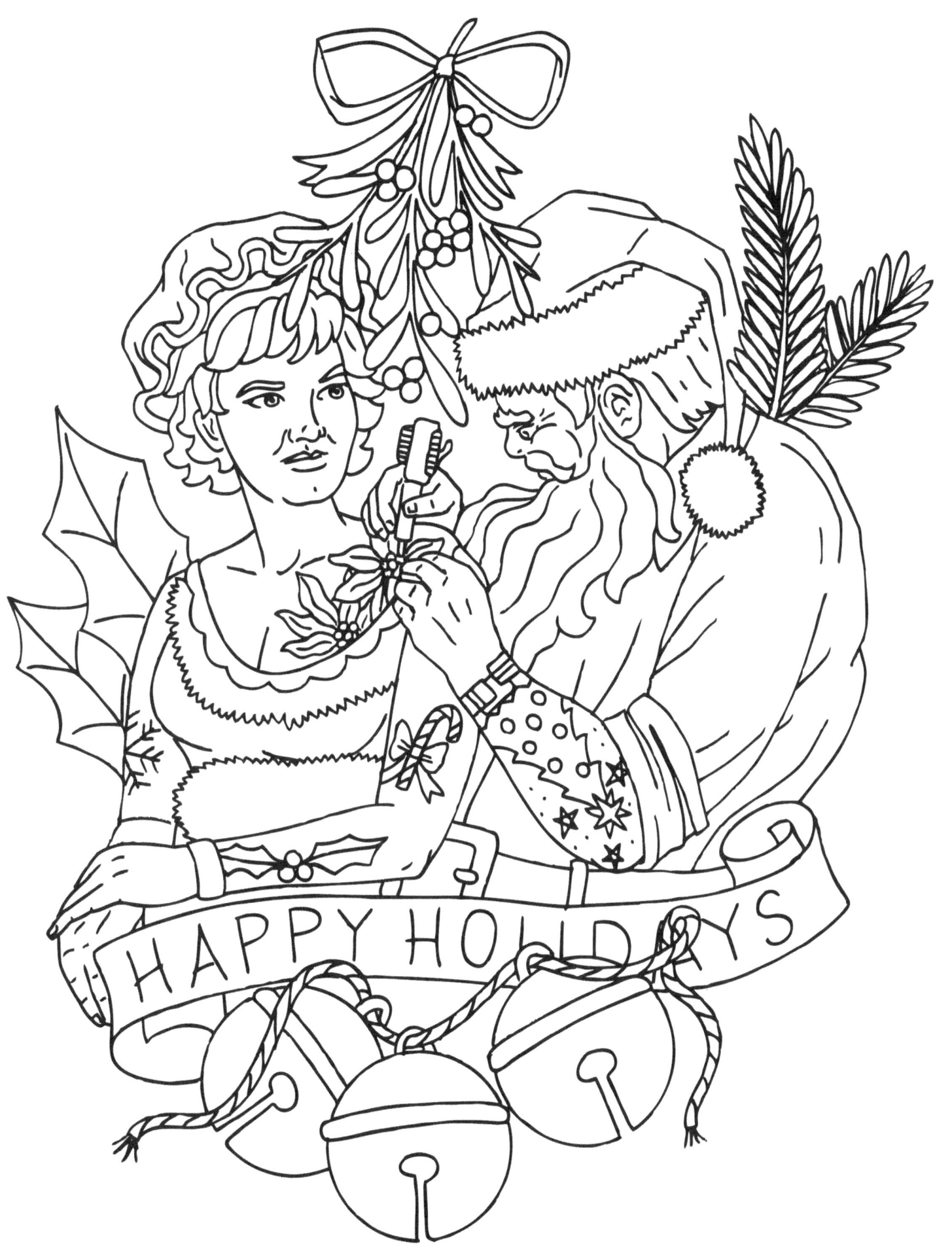

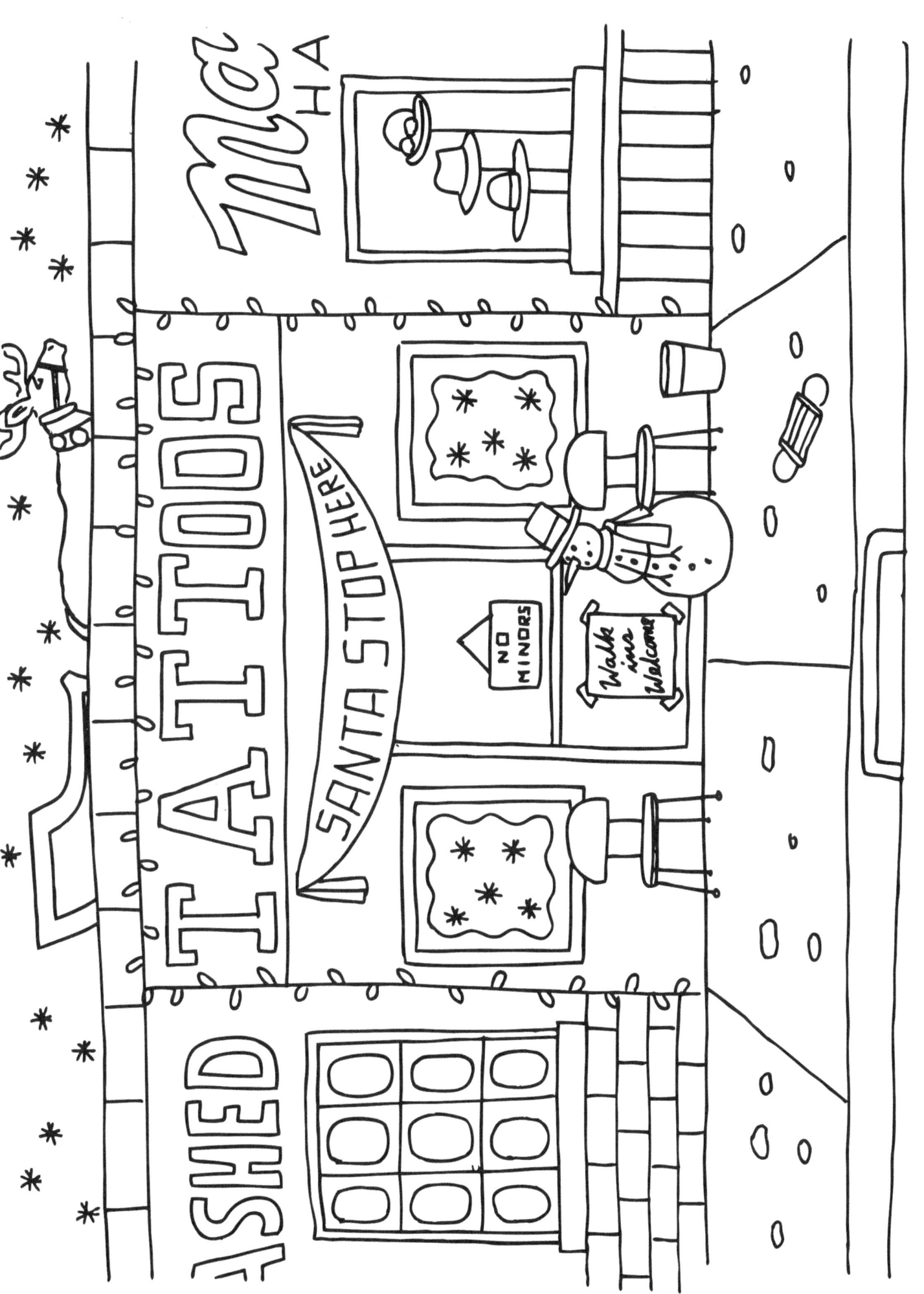

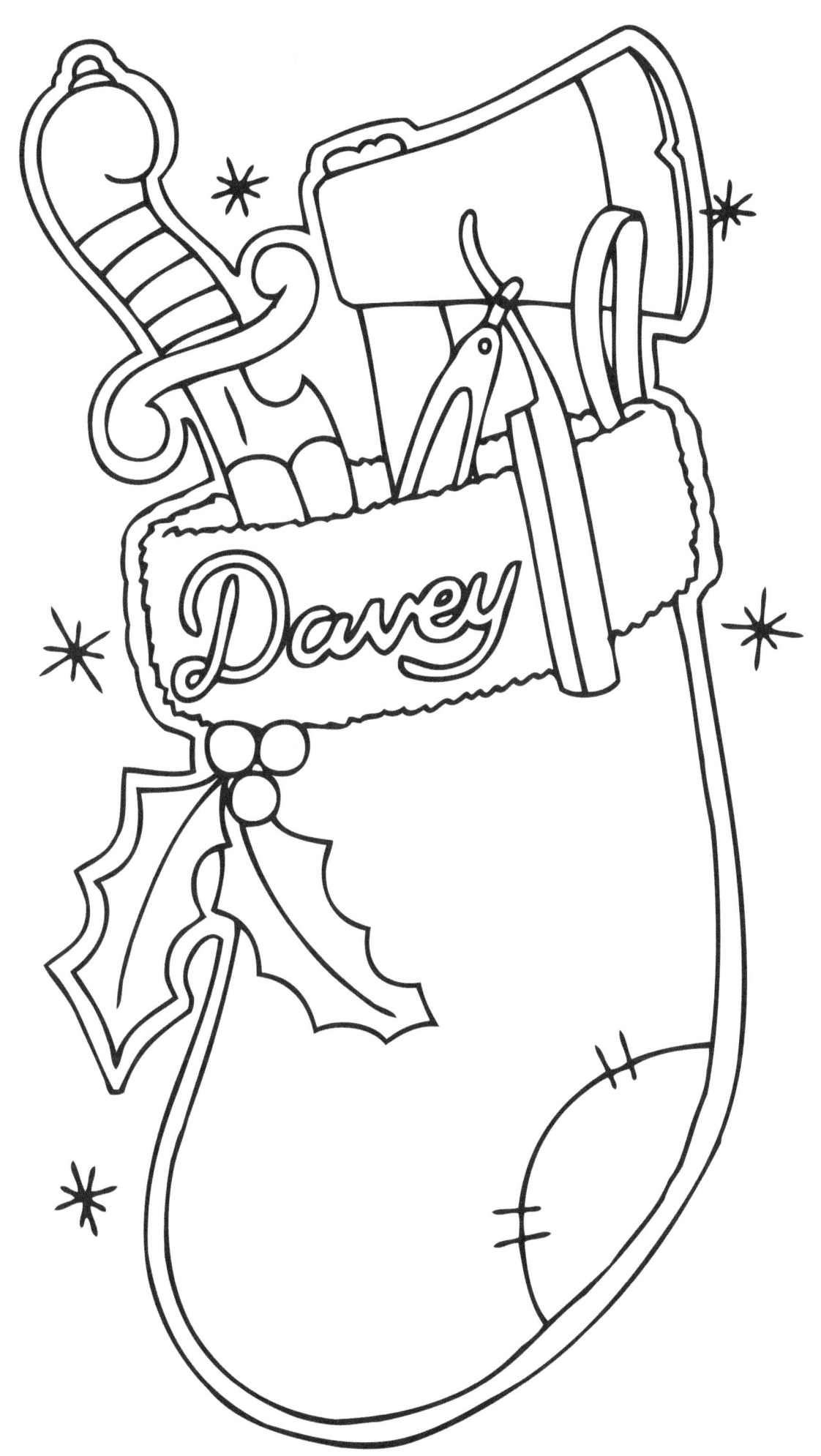

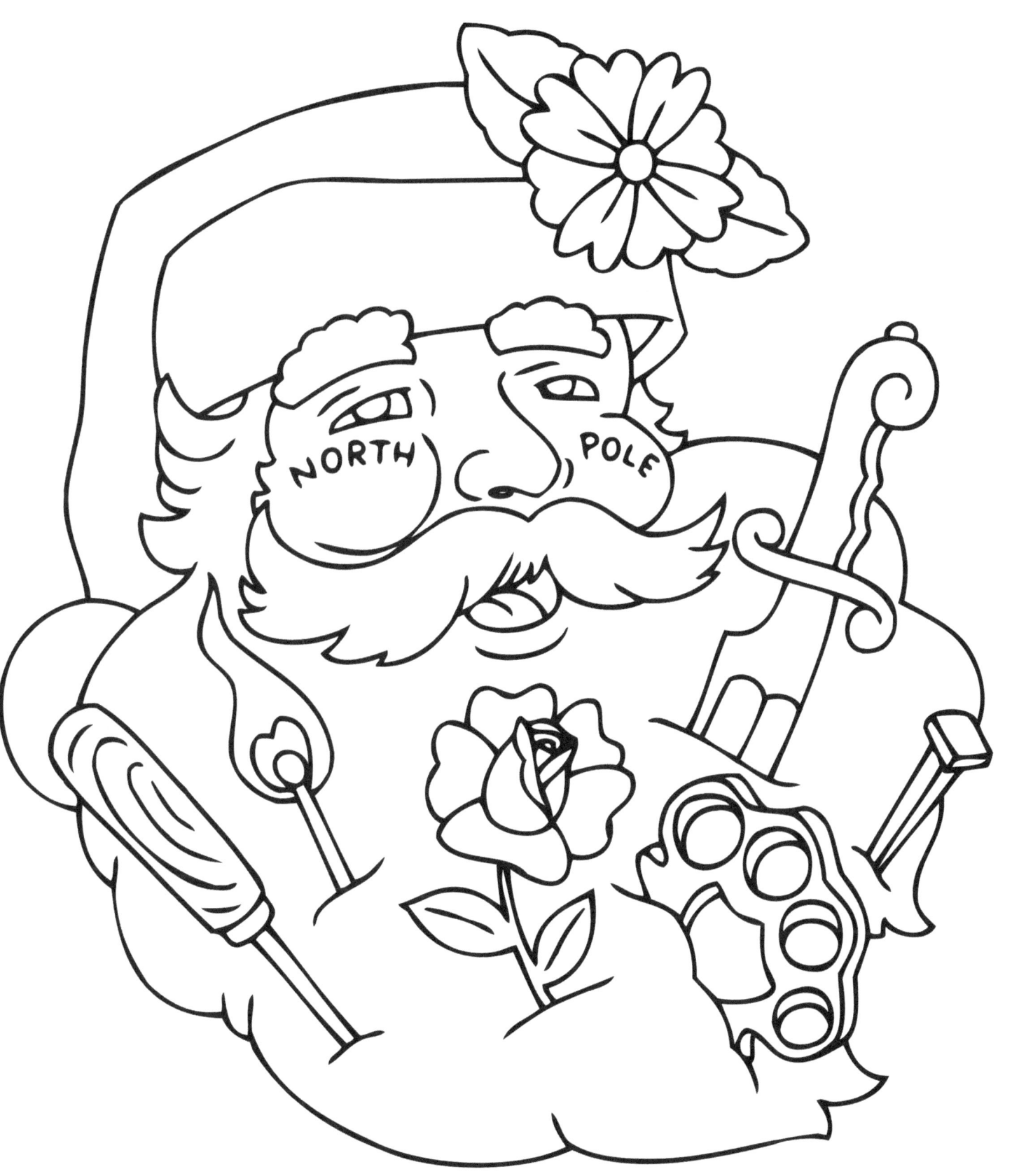

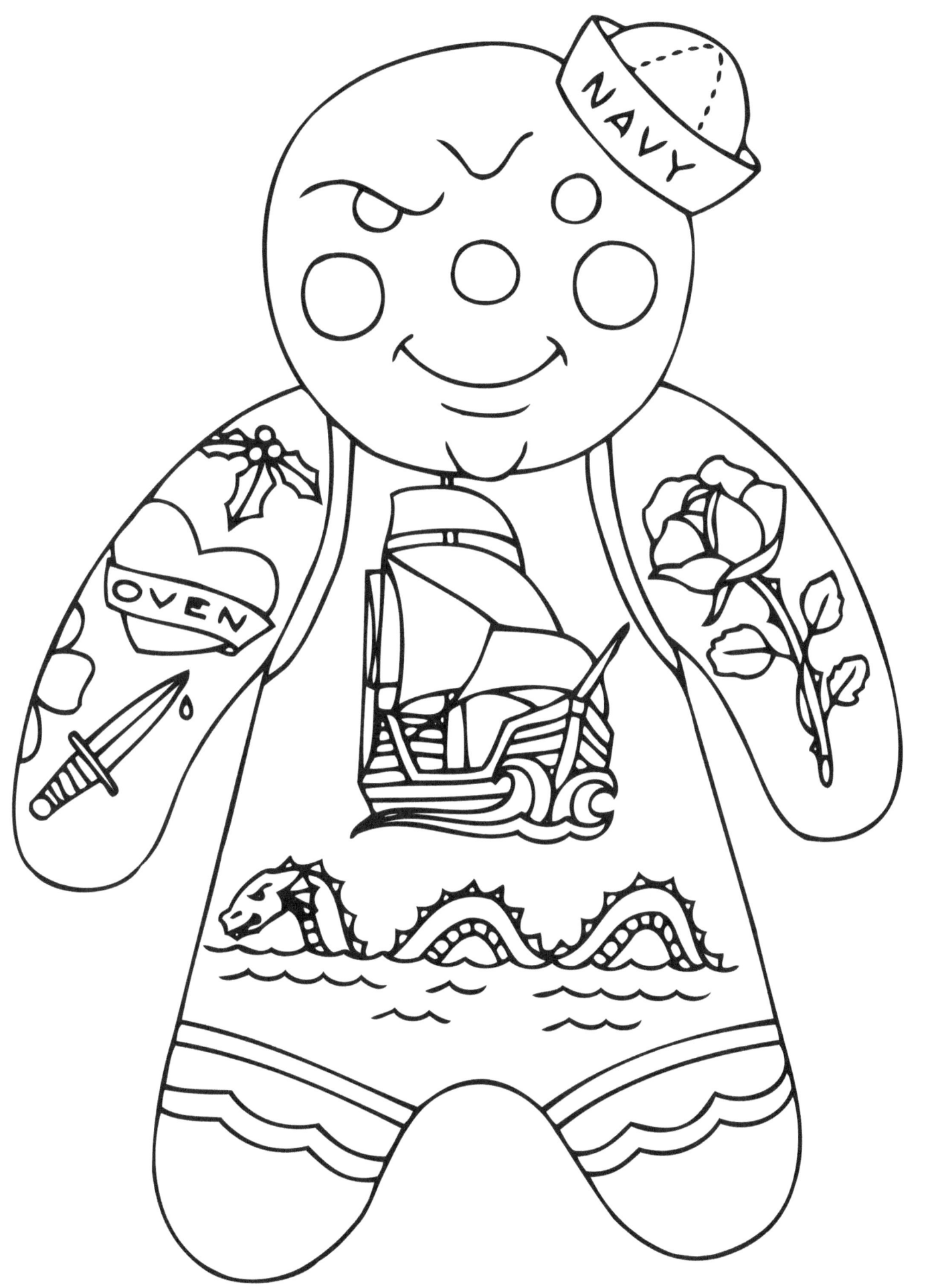

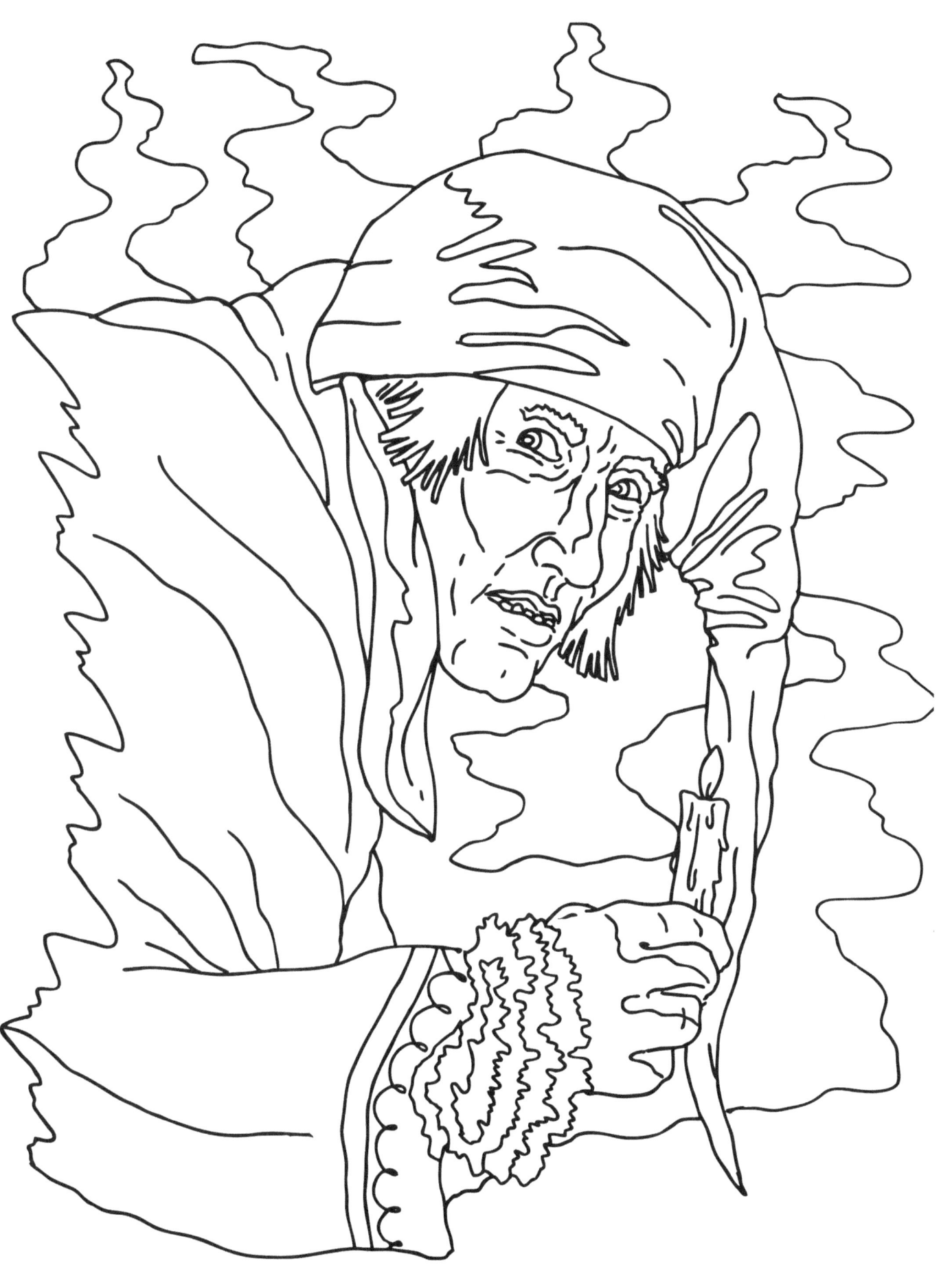

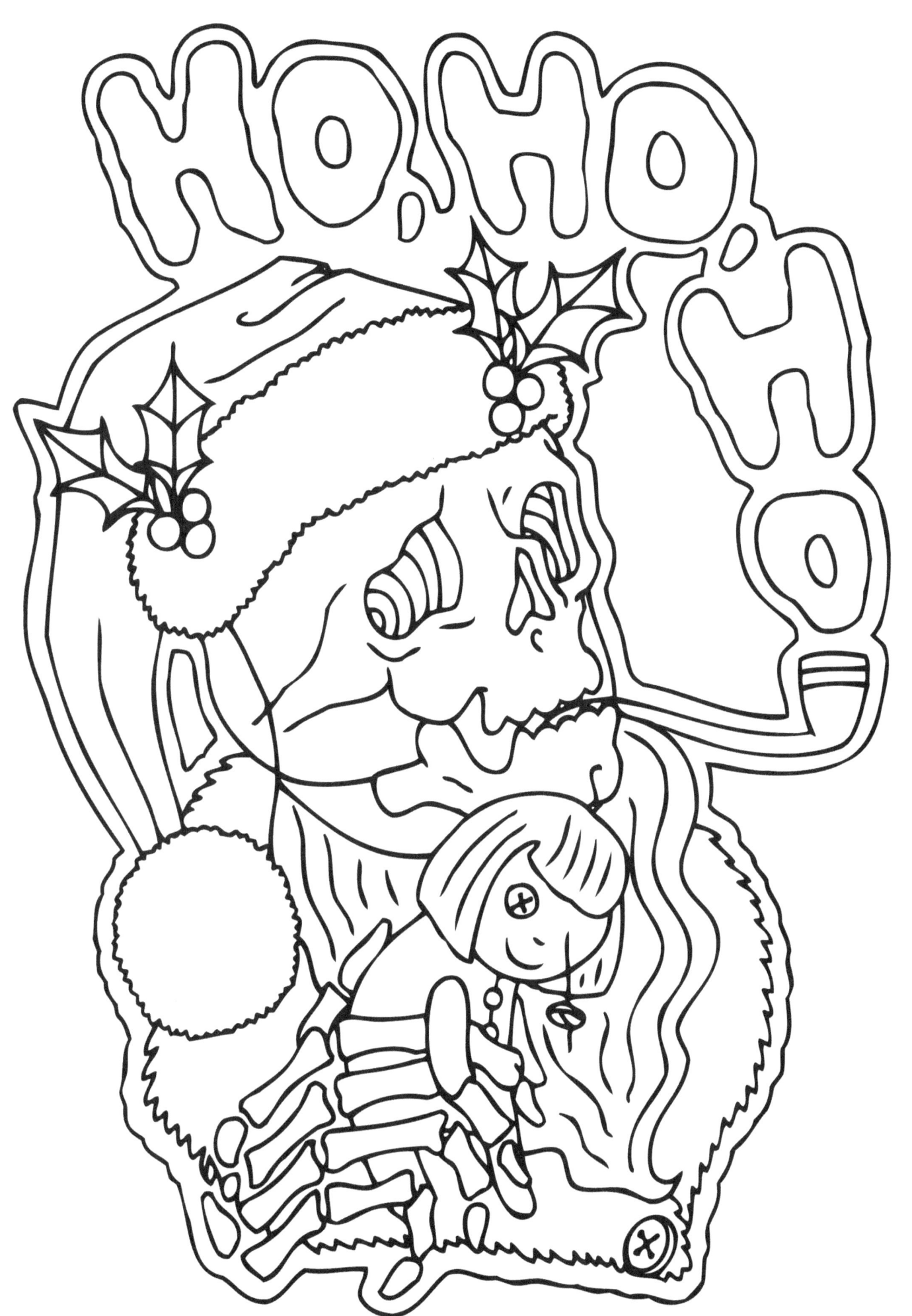

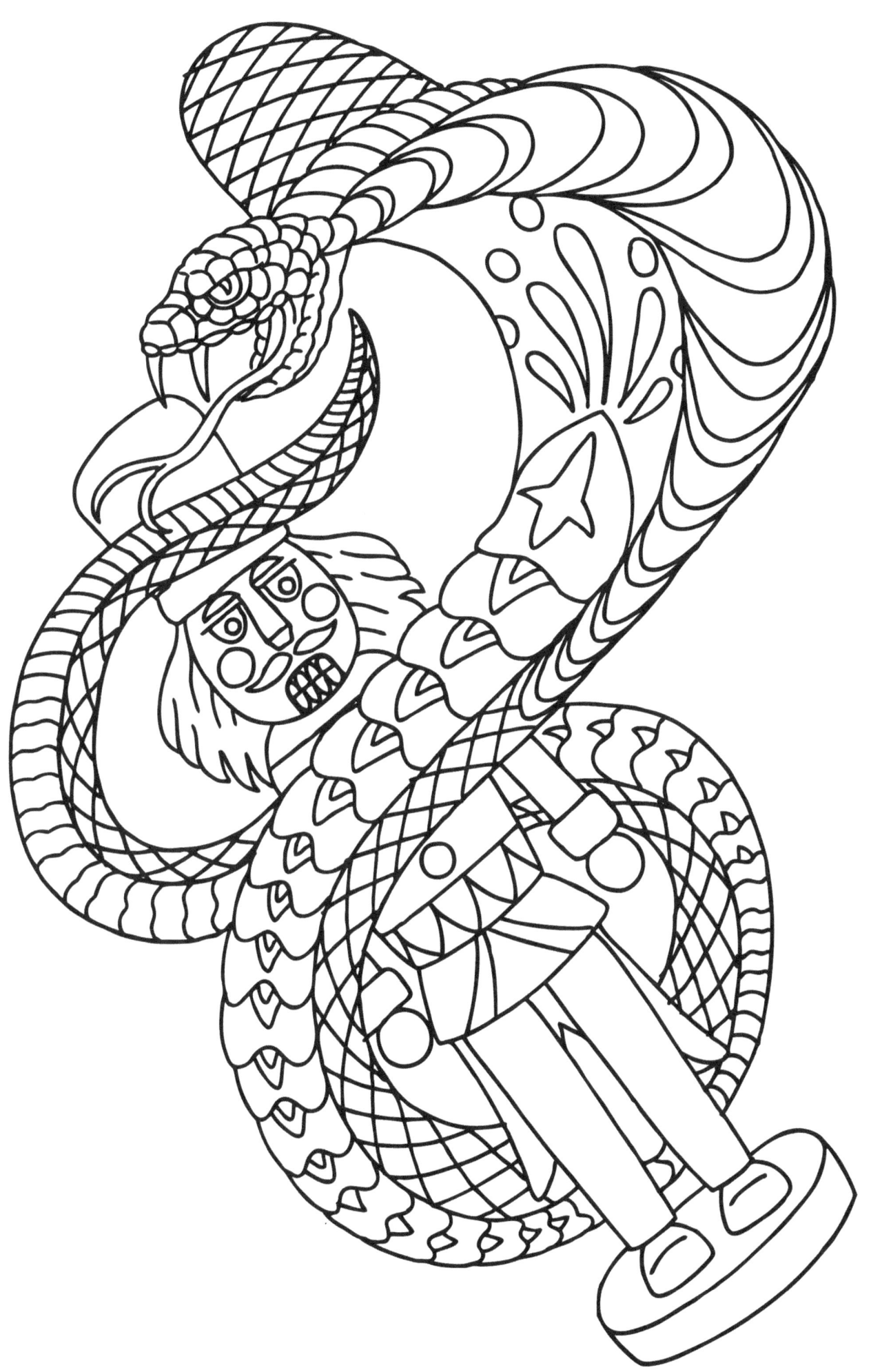

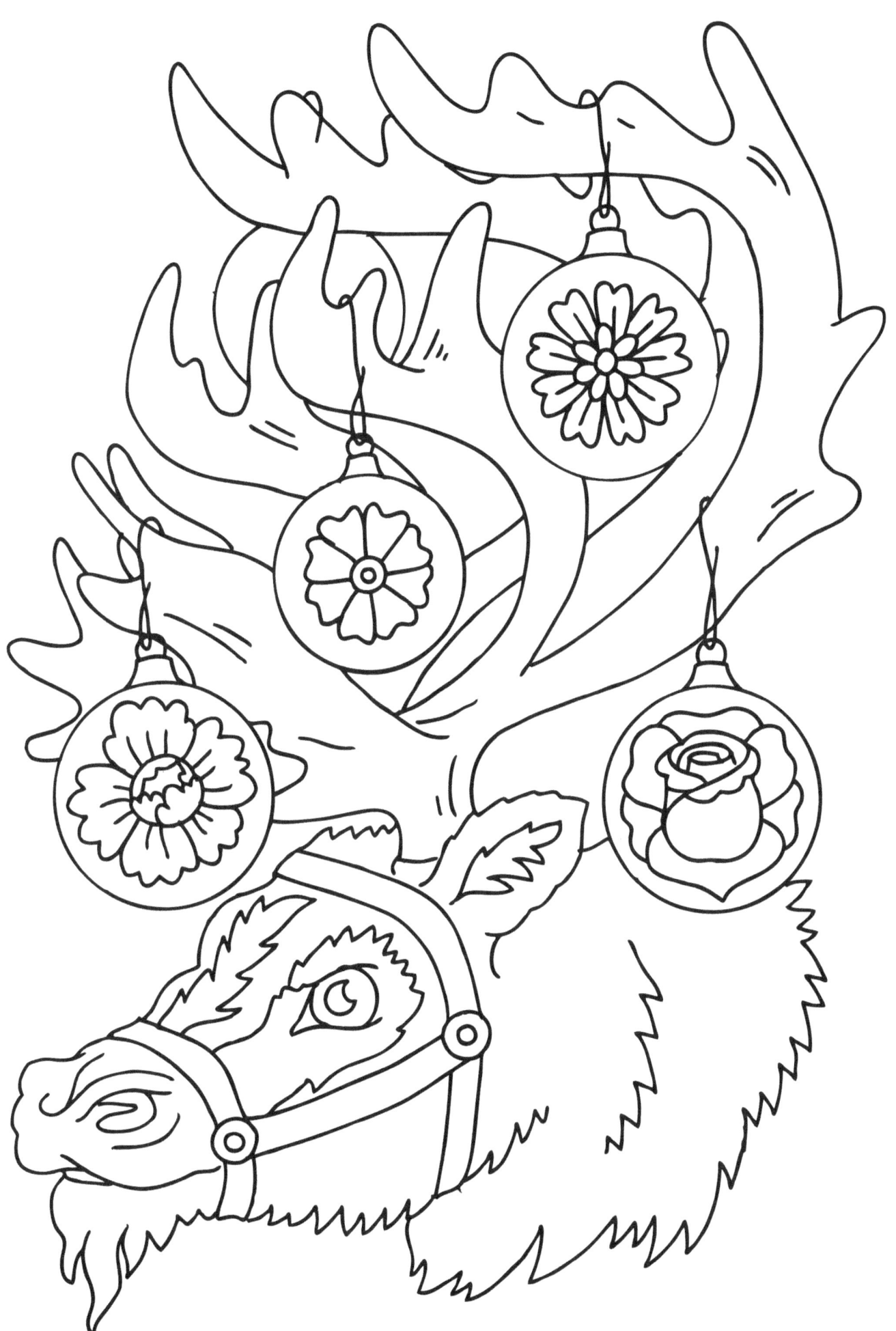

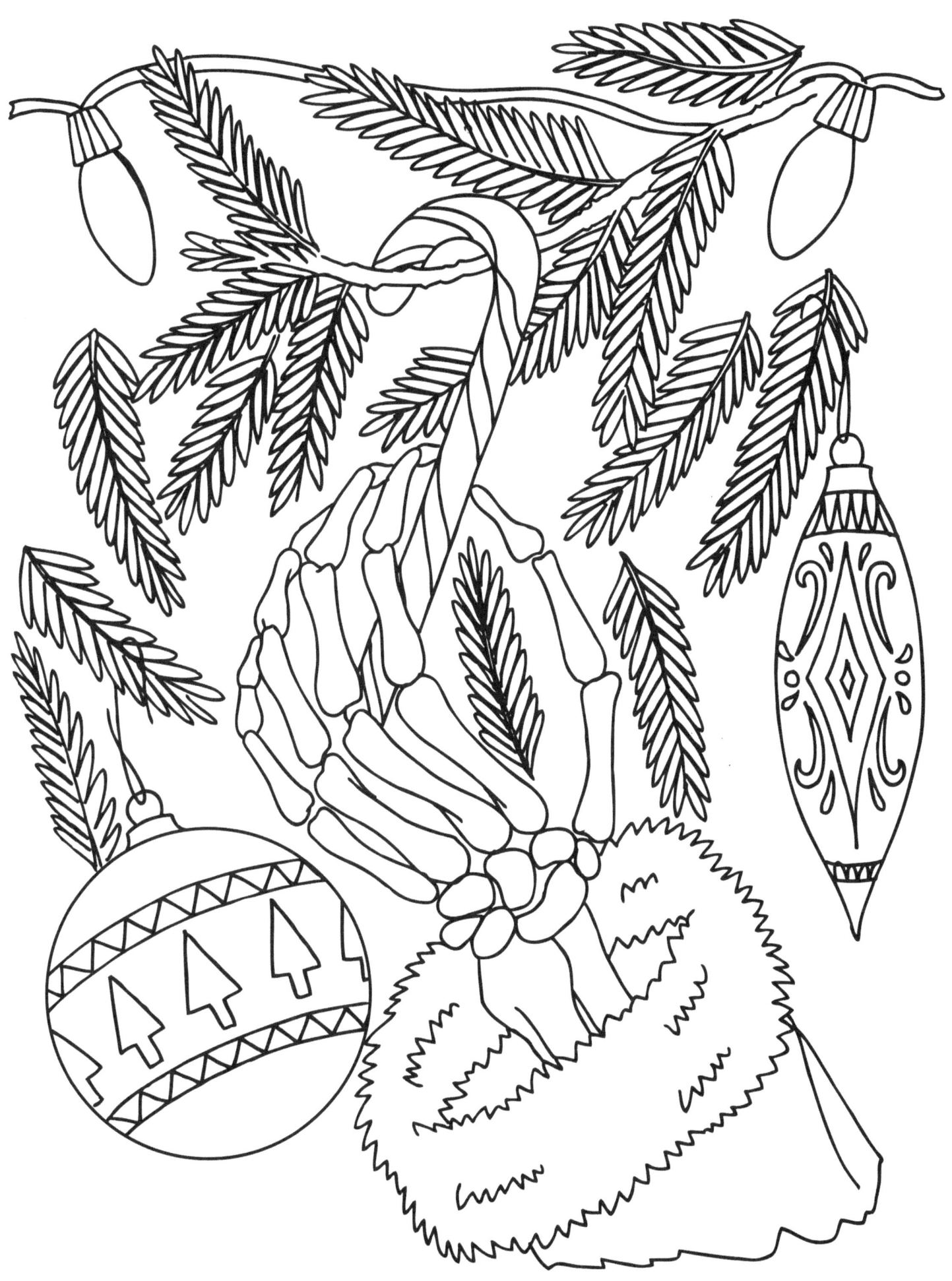

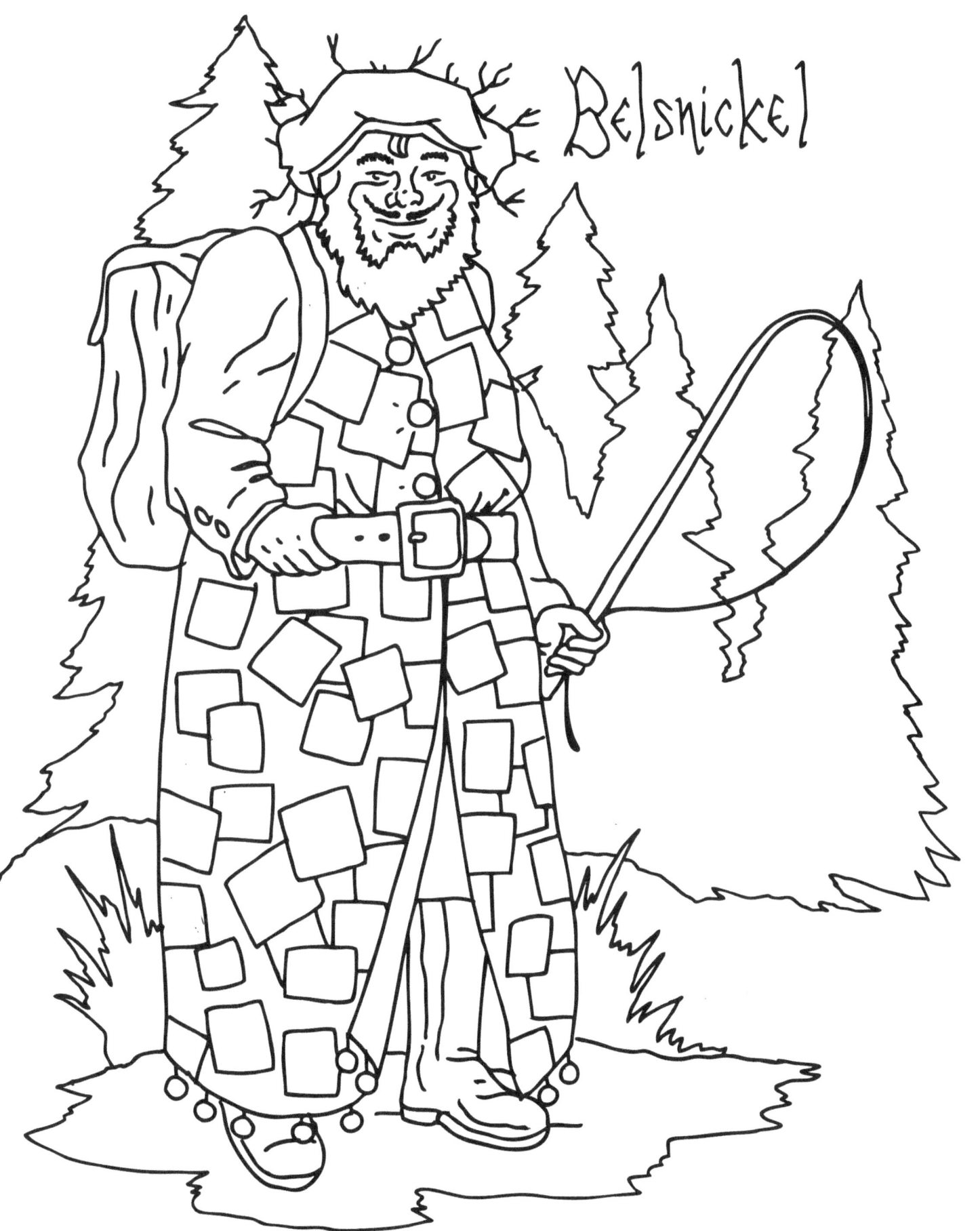

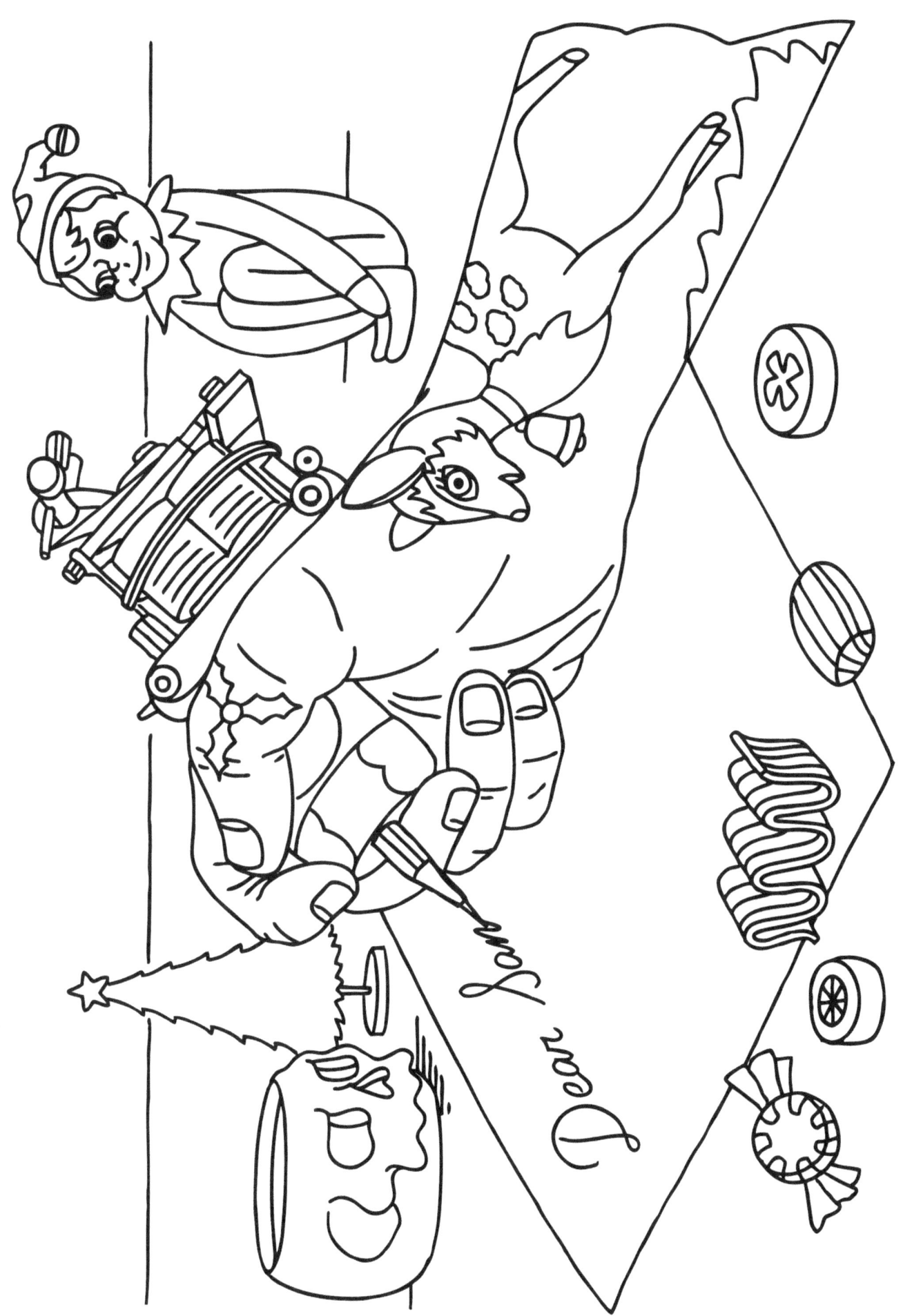

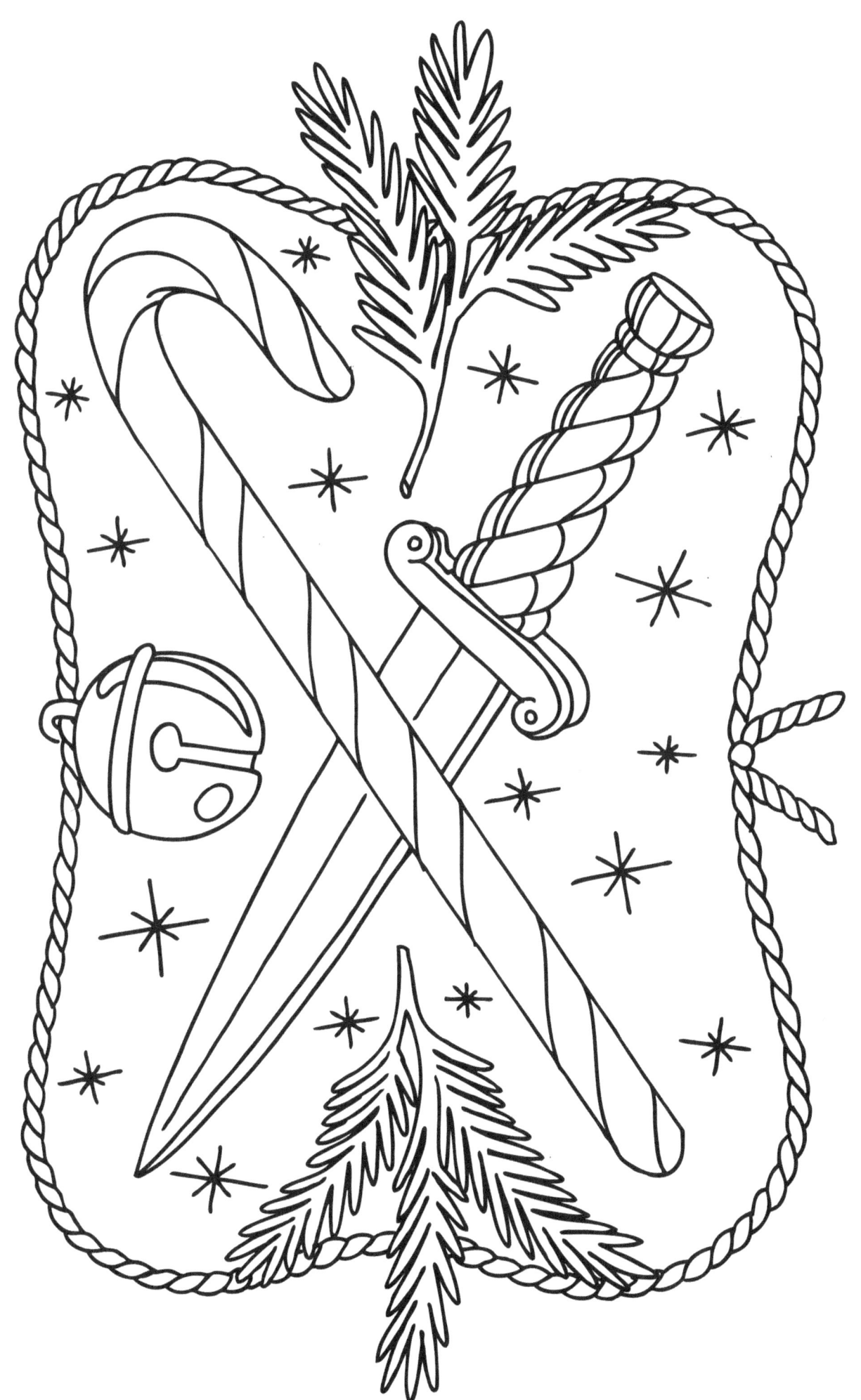

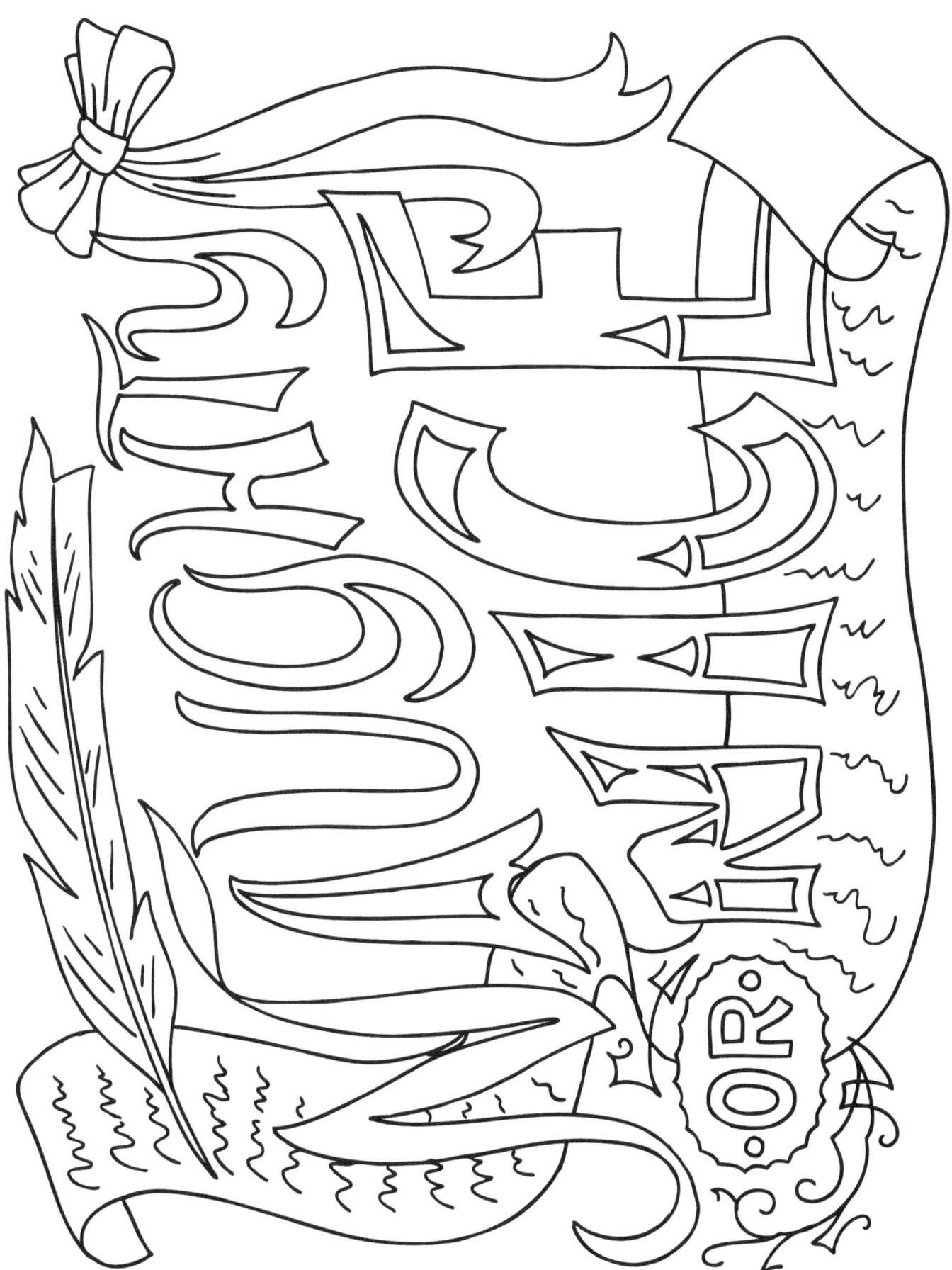

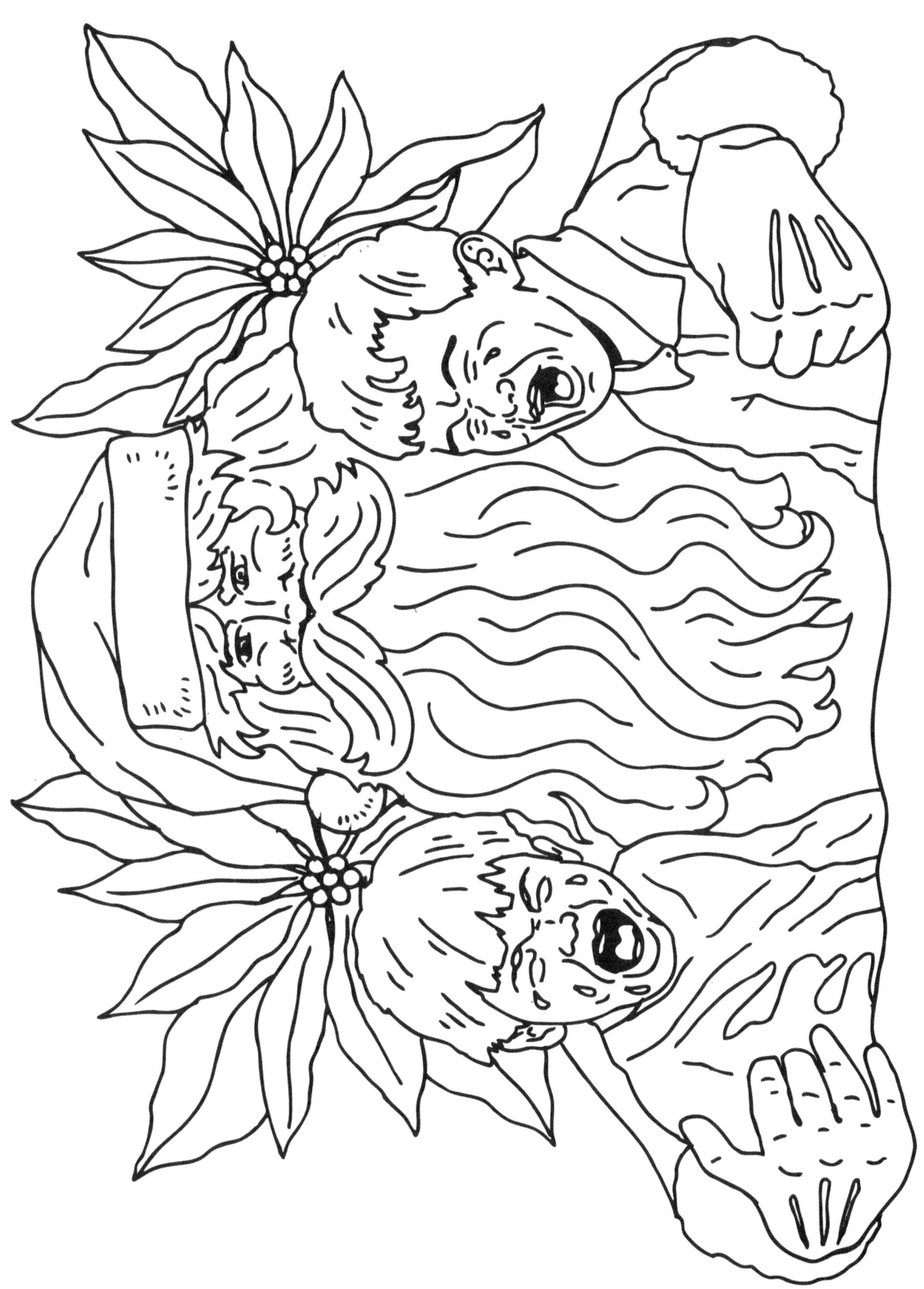

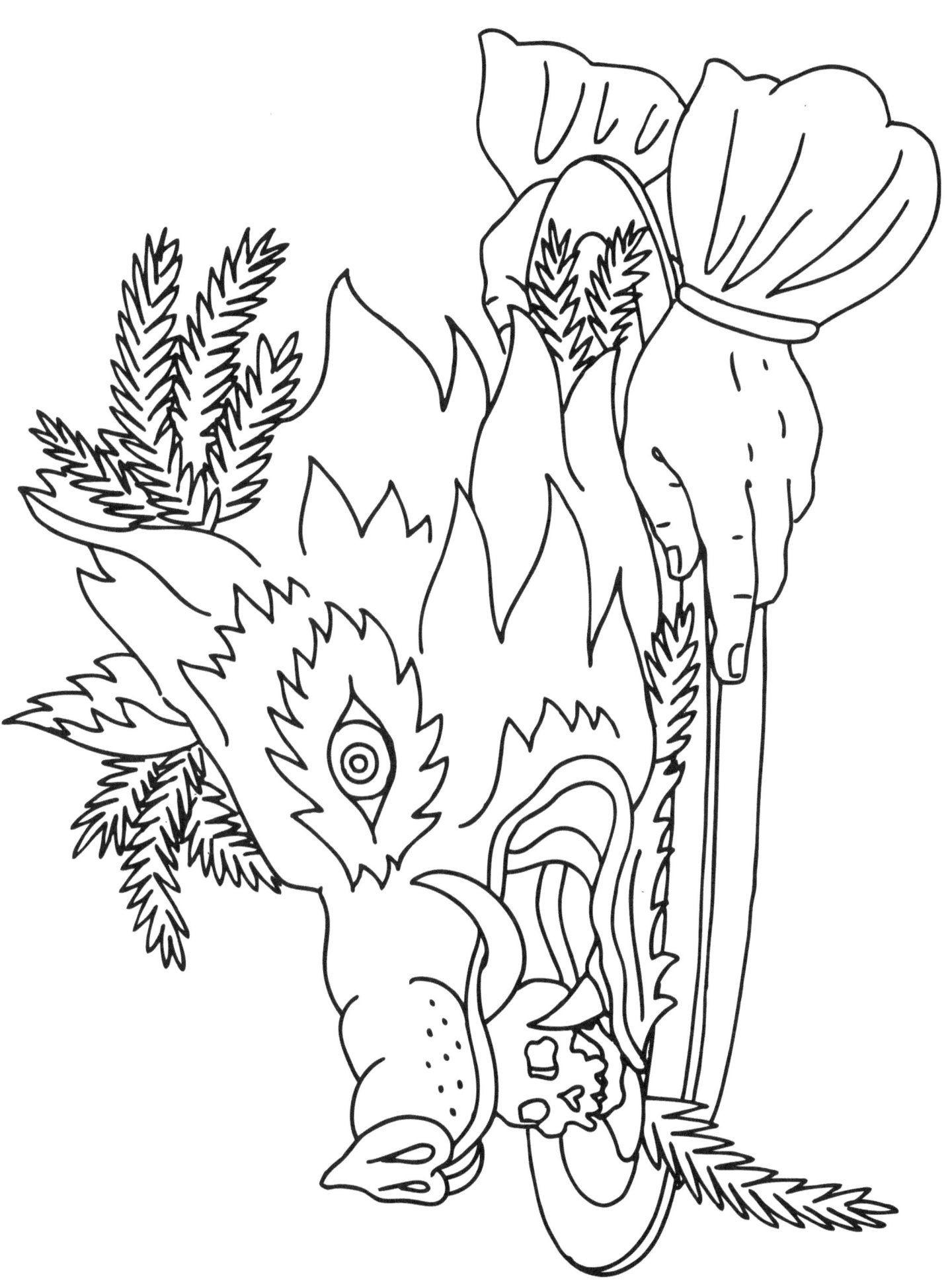

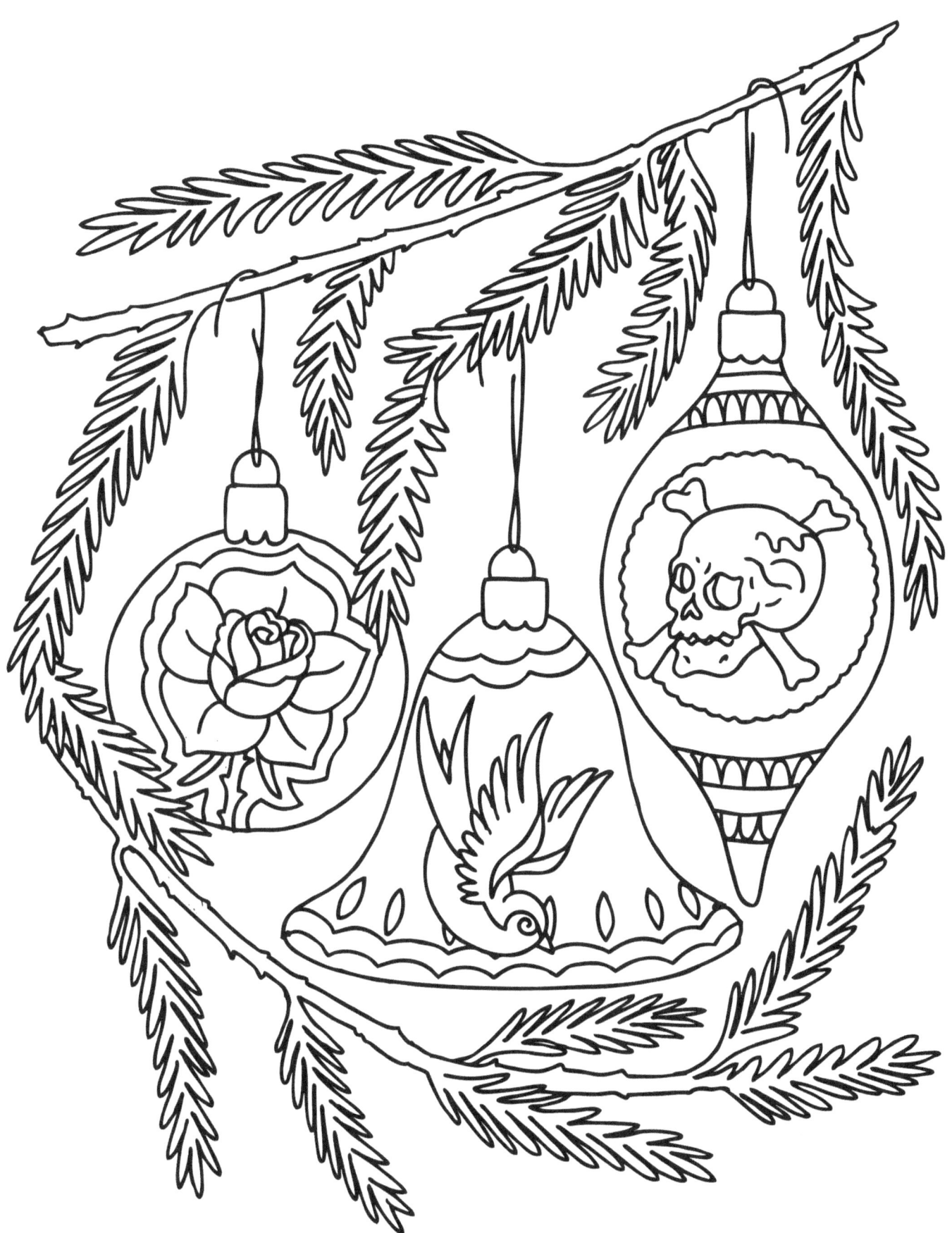

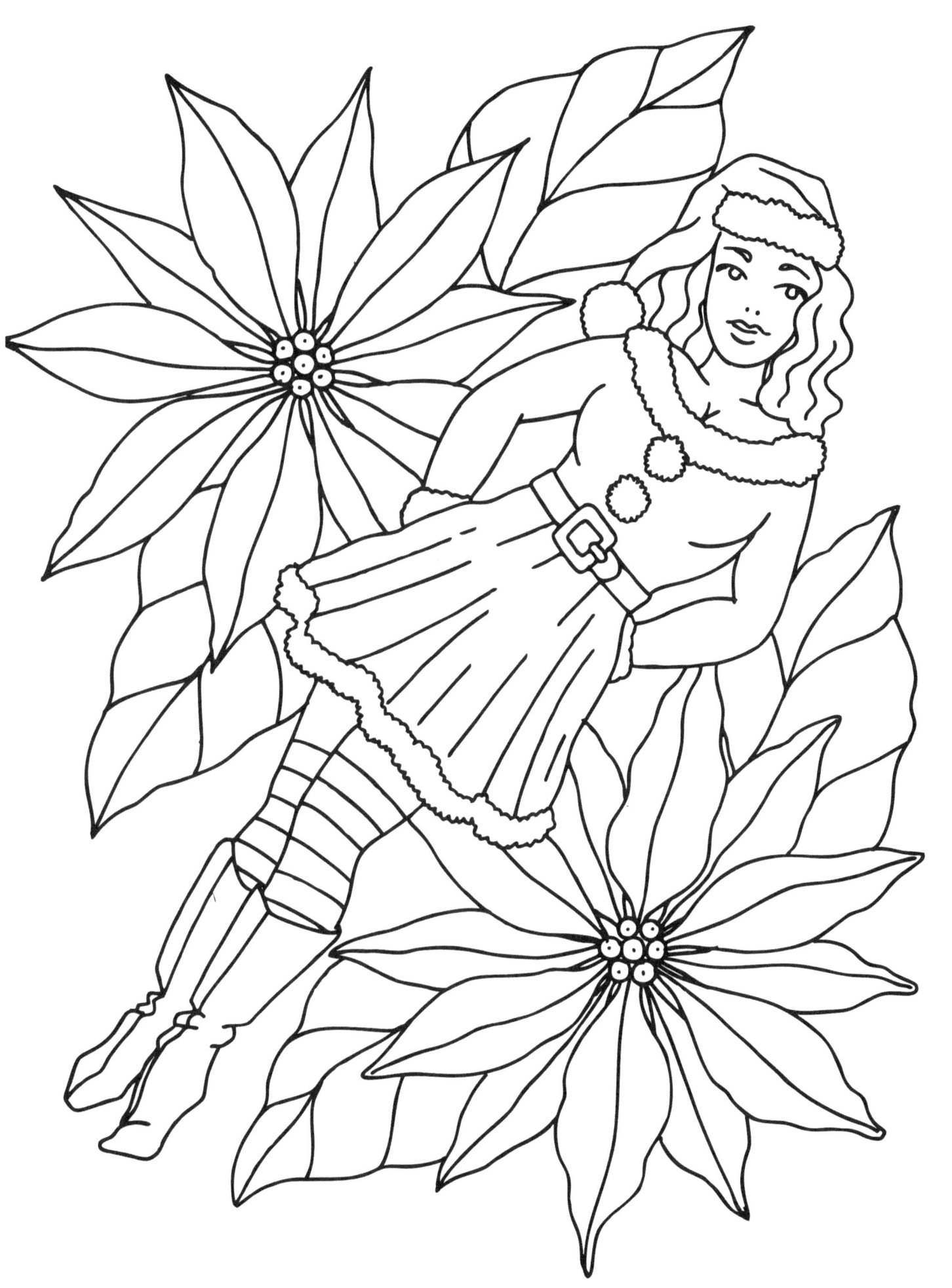

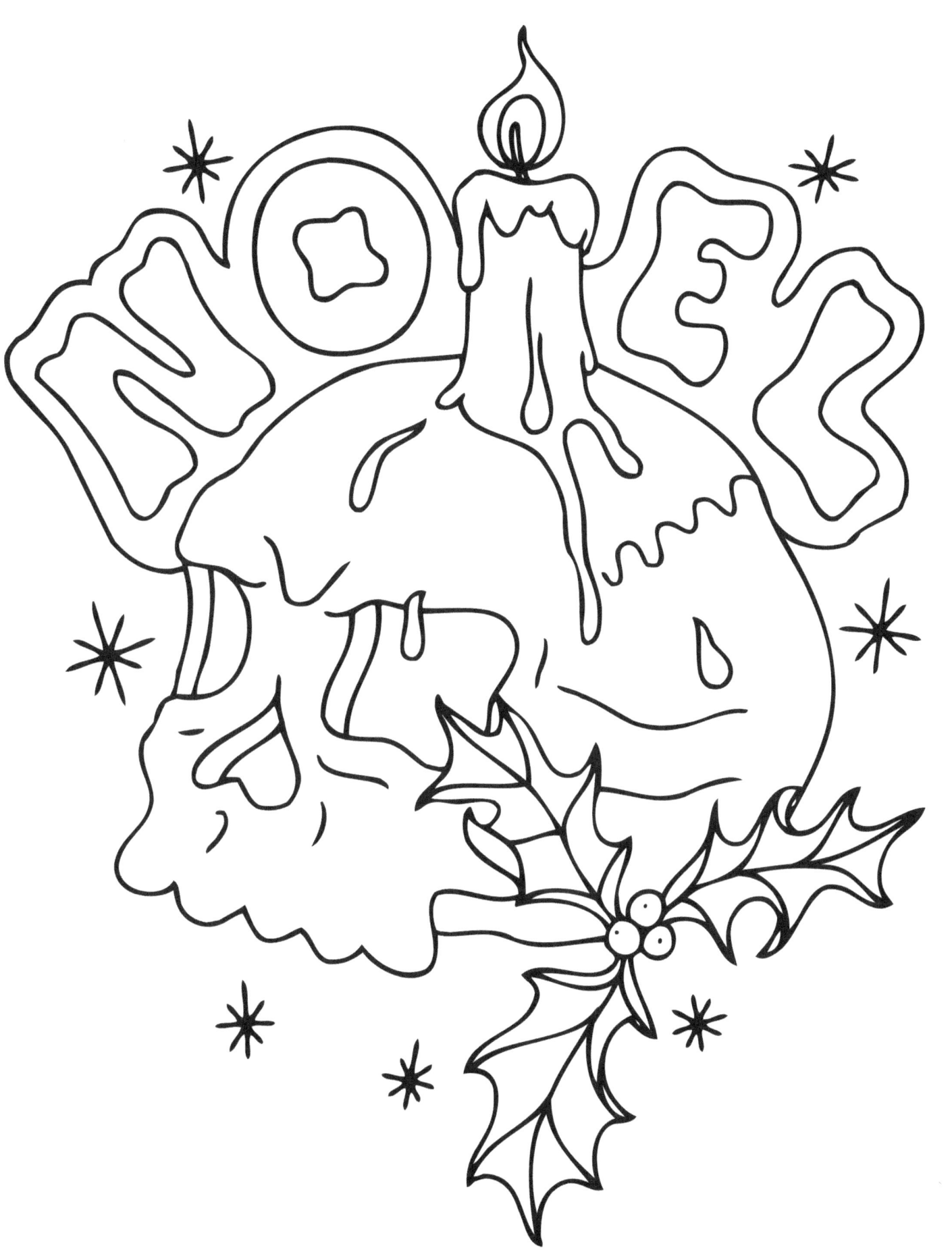

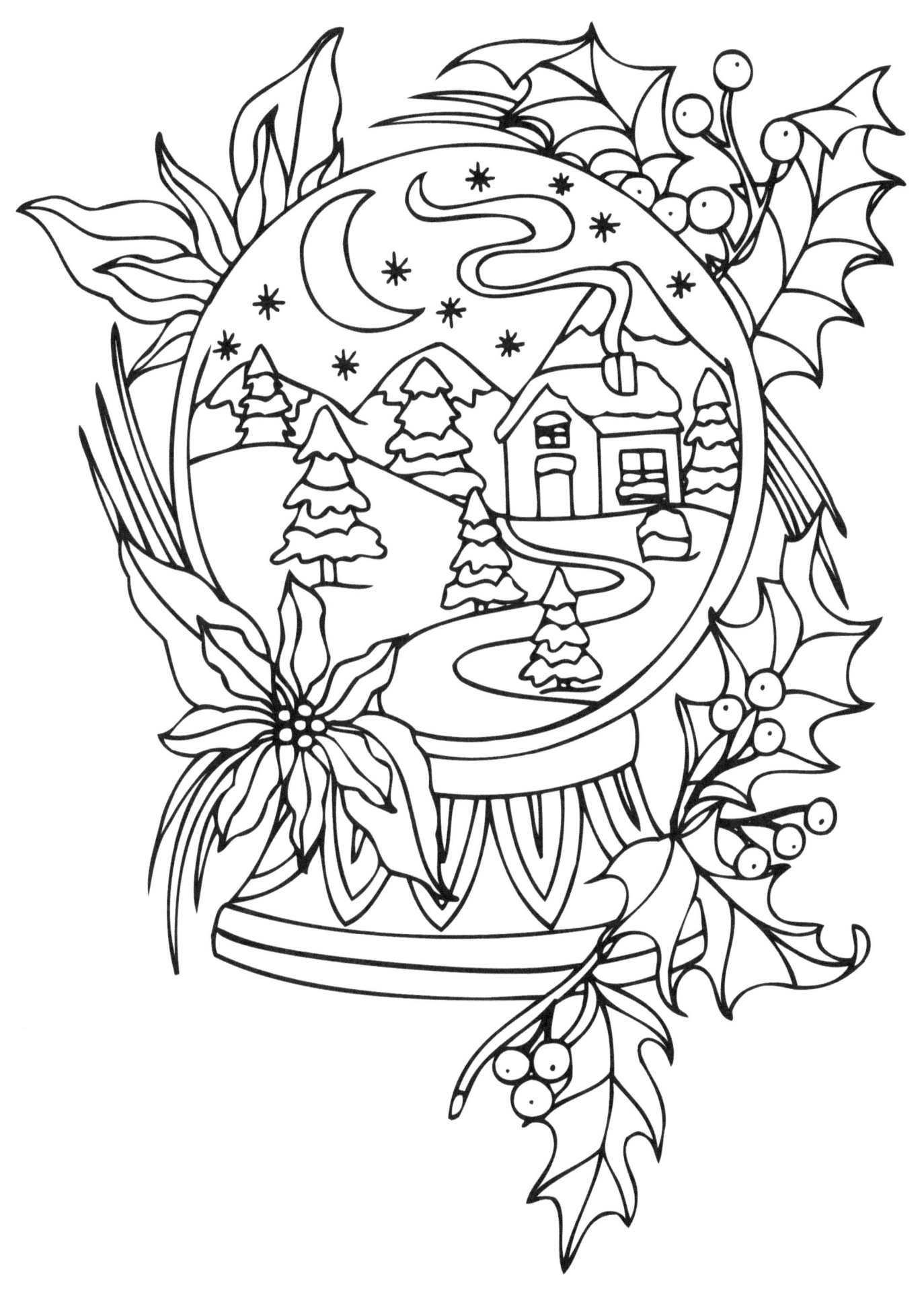

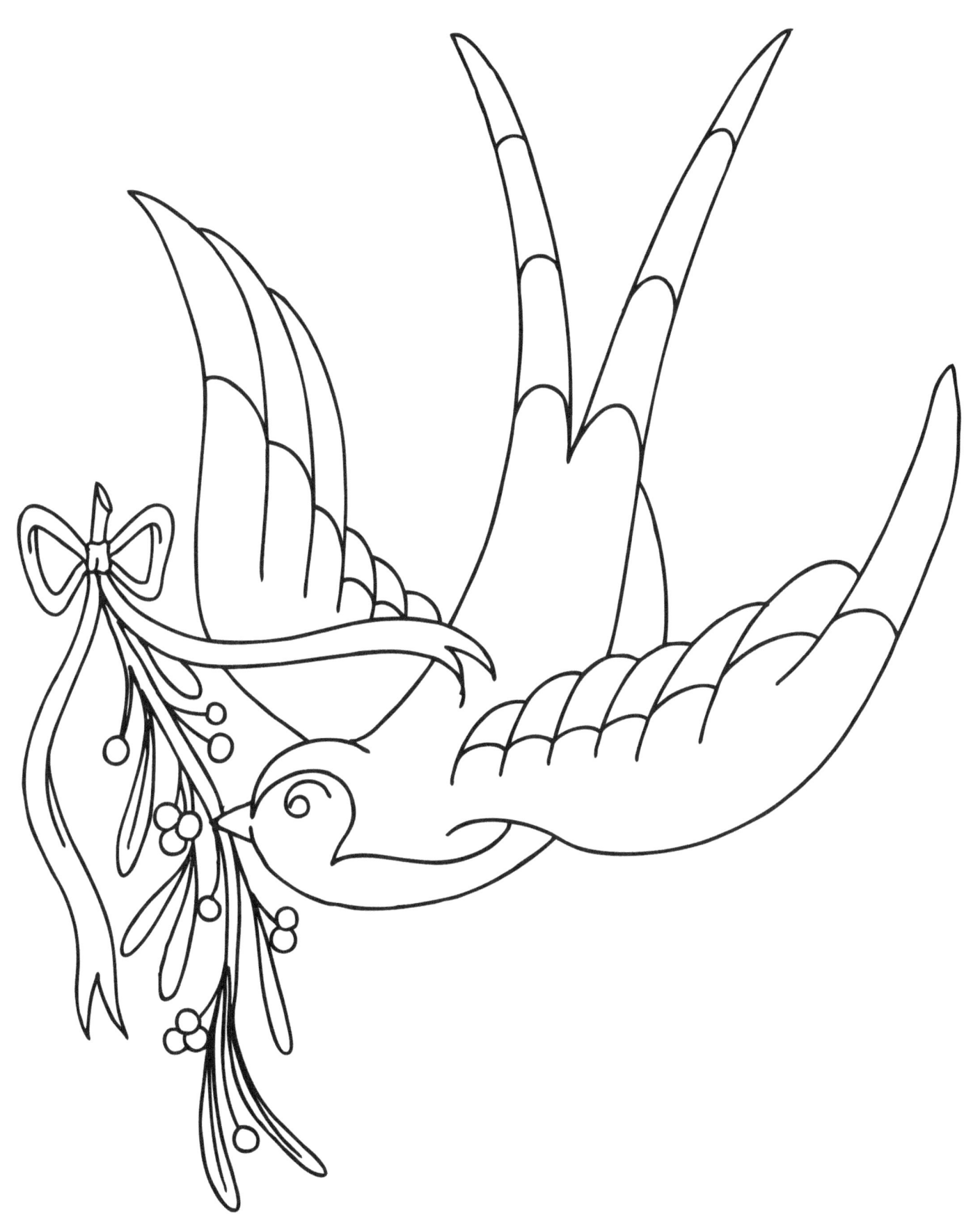

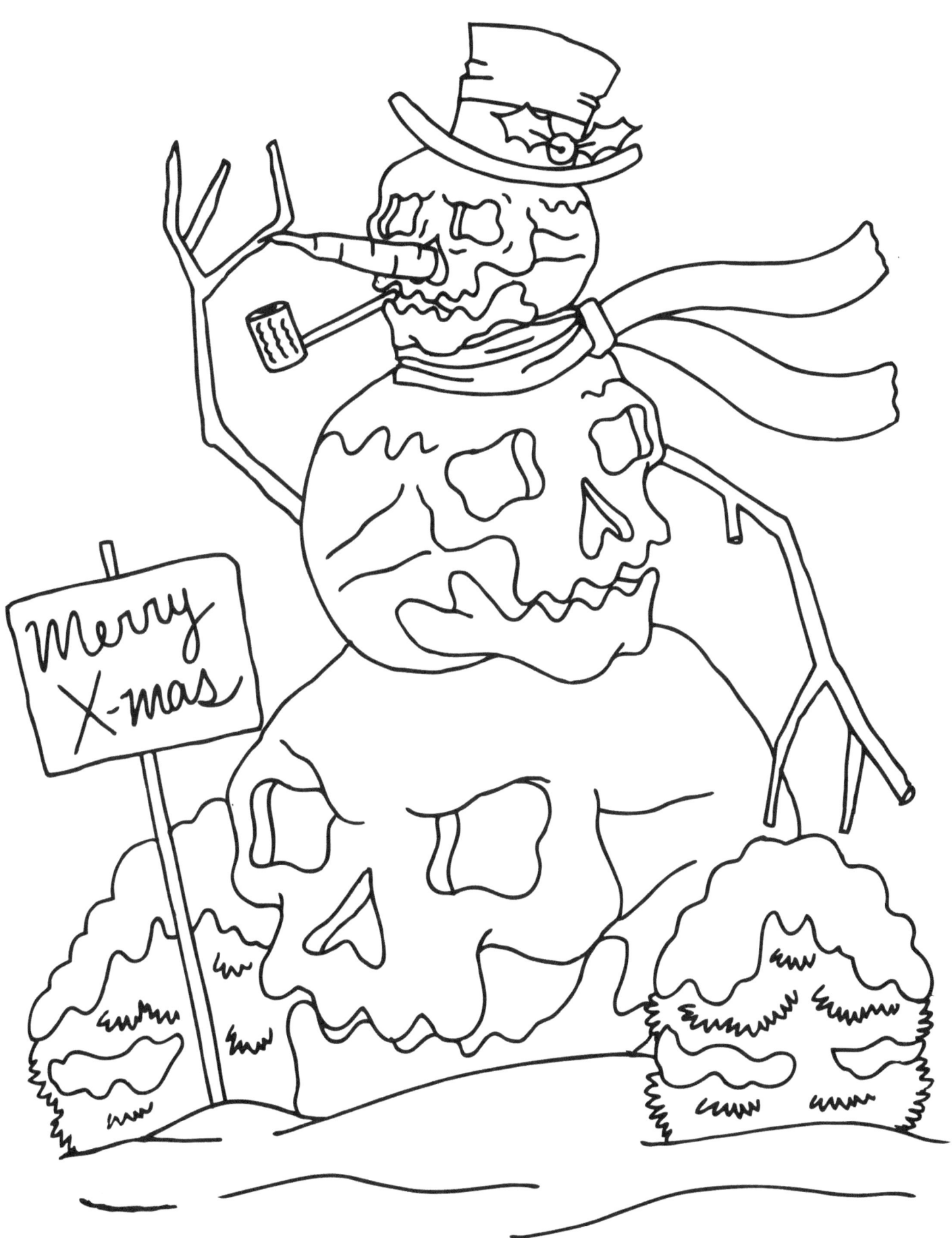

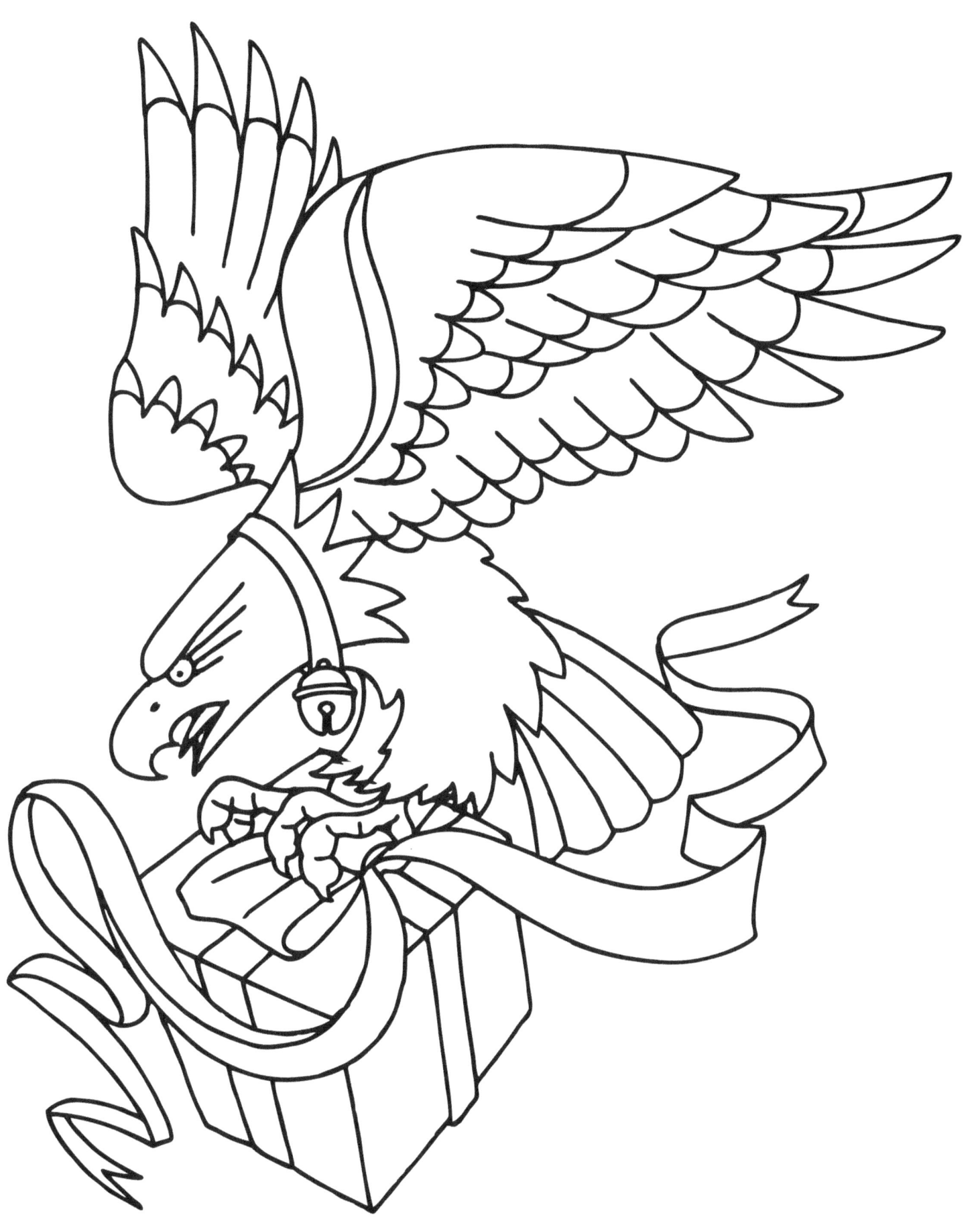

ENJOY
10 PAGES FROM OUR

TRADITIONAL TATTOO SKULLS
COLORING BOOK

AVAILABLE ON AMAZON.

SEARCH
"STEAL THIS FLASH"
FOR ALL OF OUR TITLES.

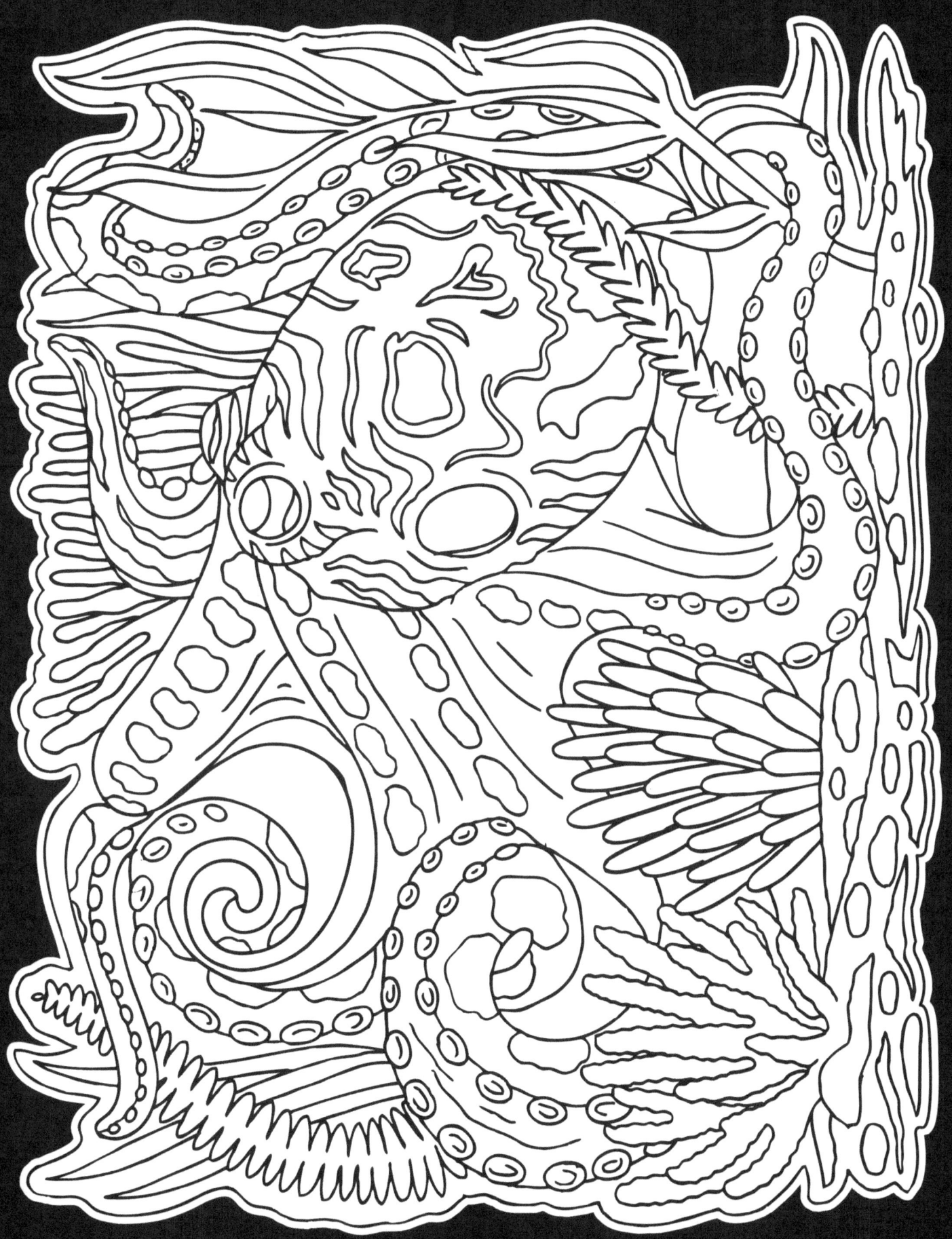

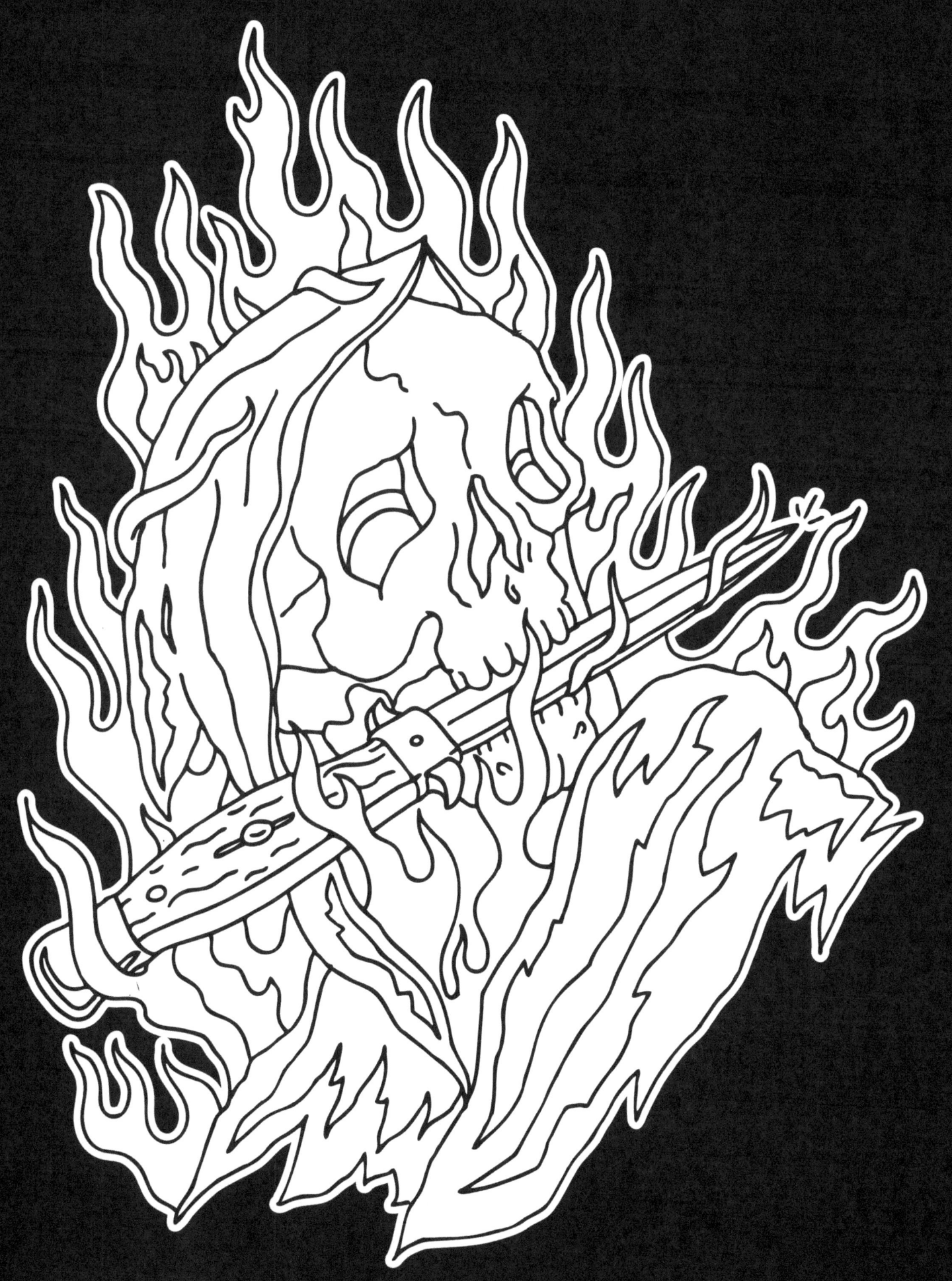

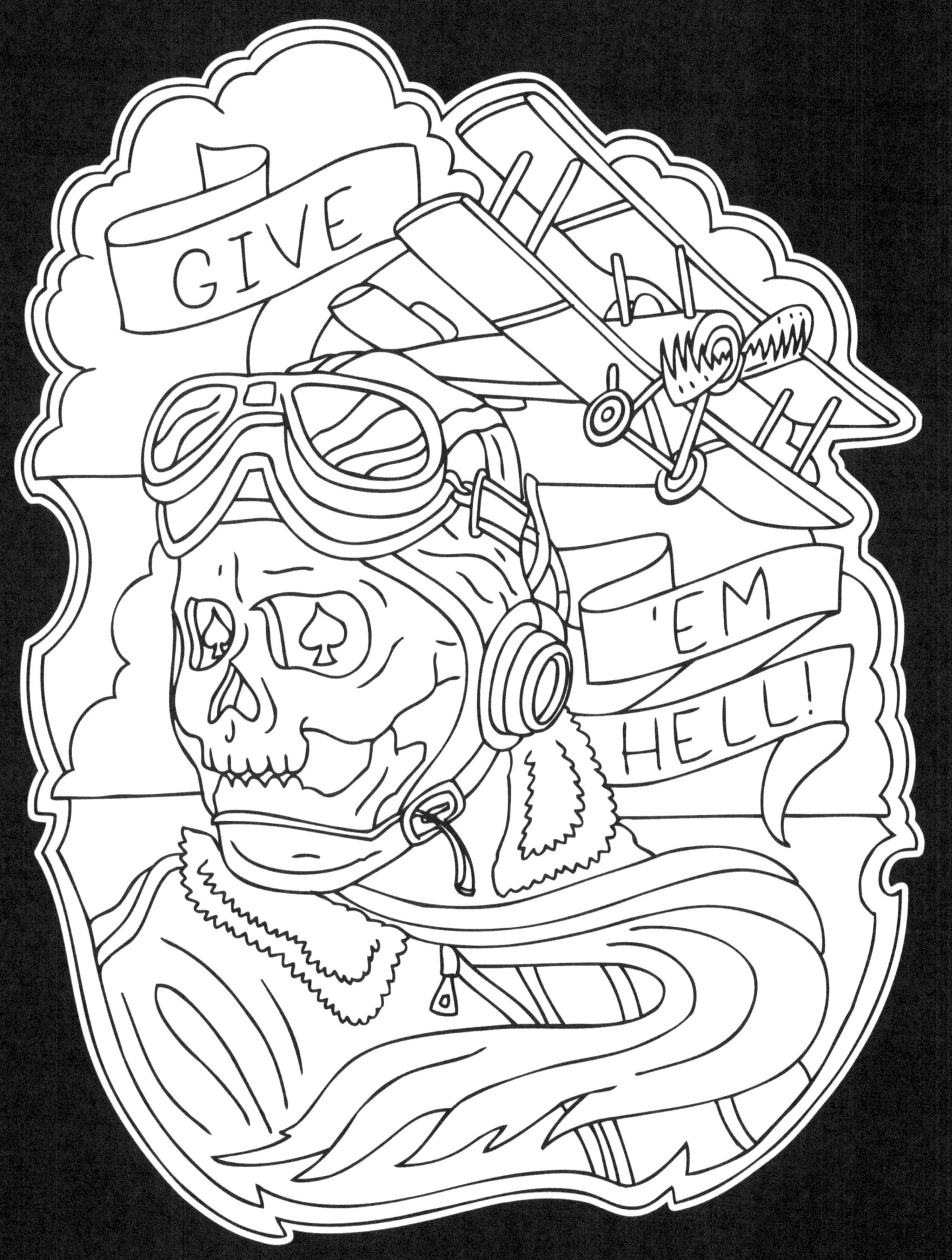

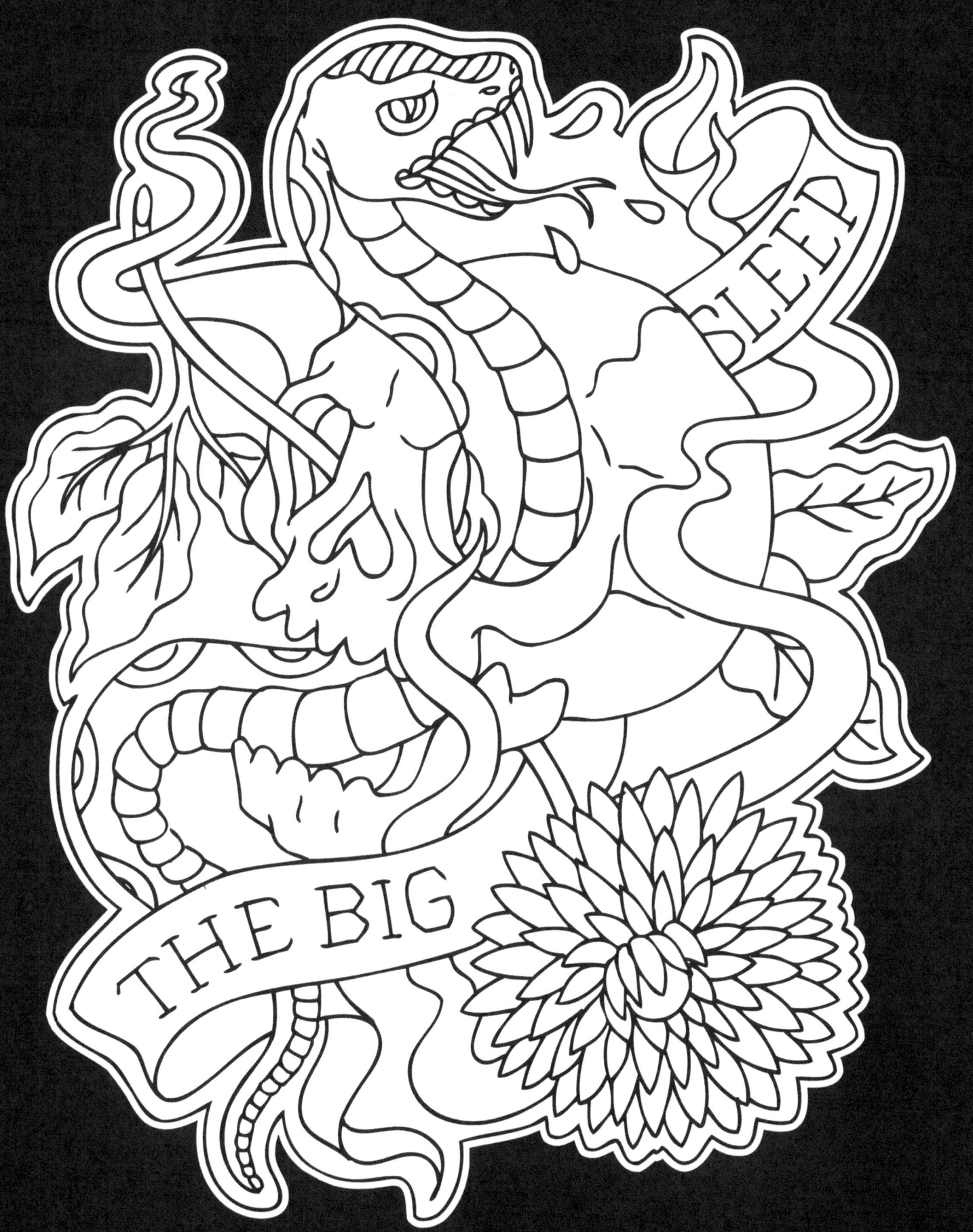

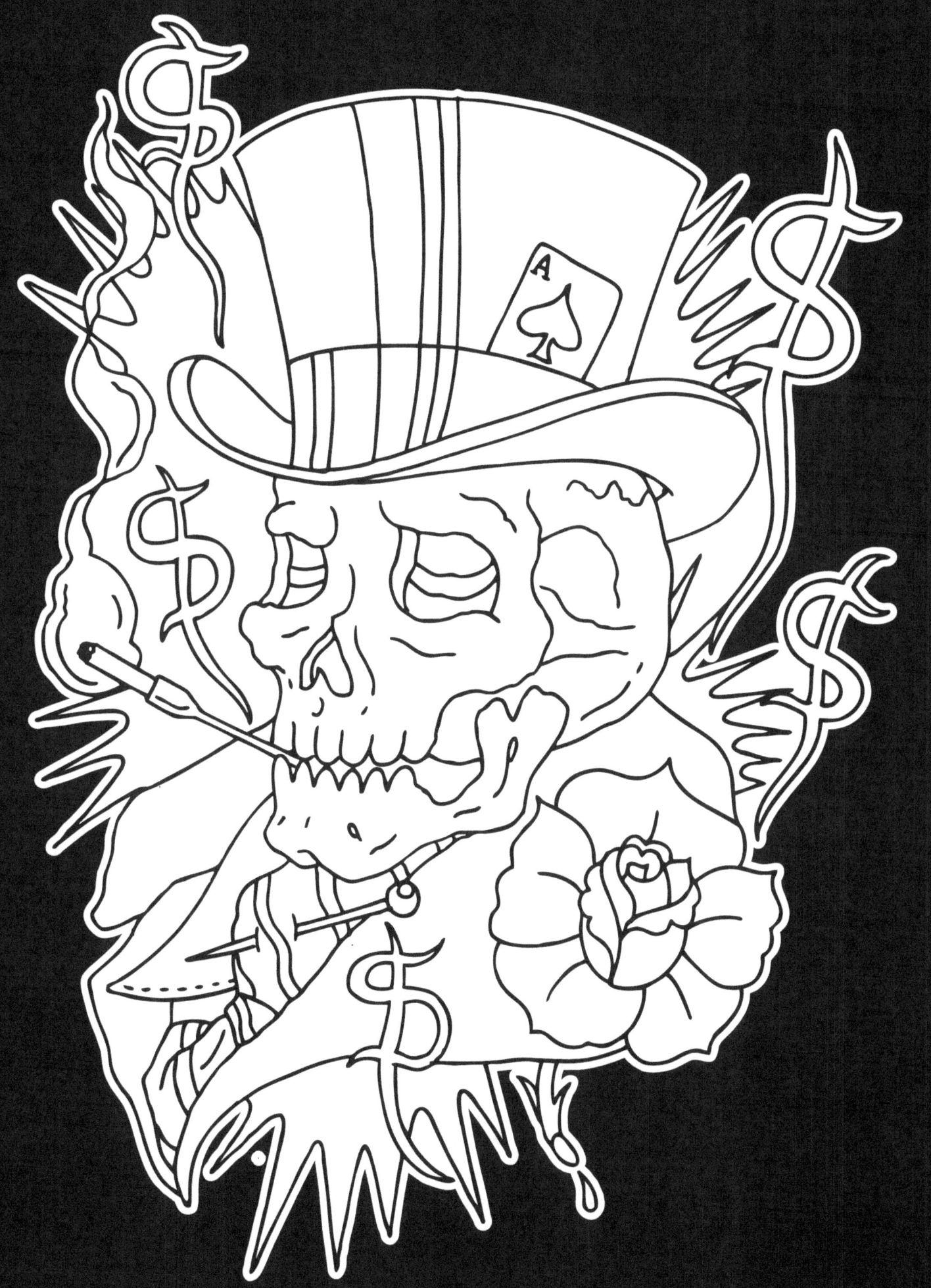

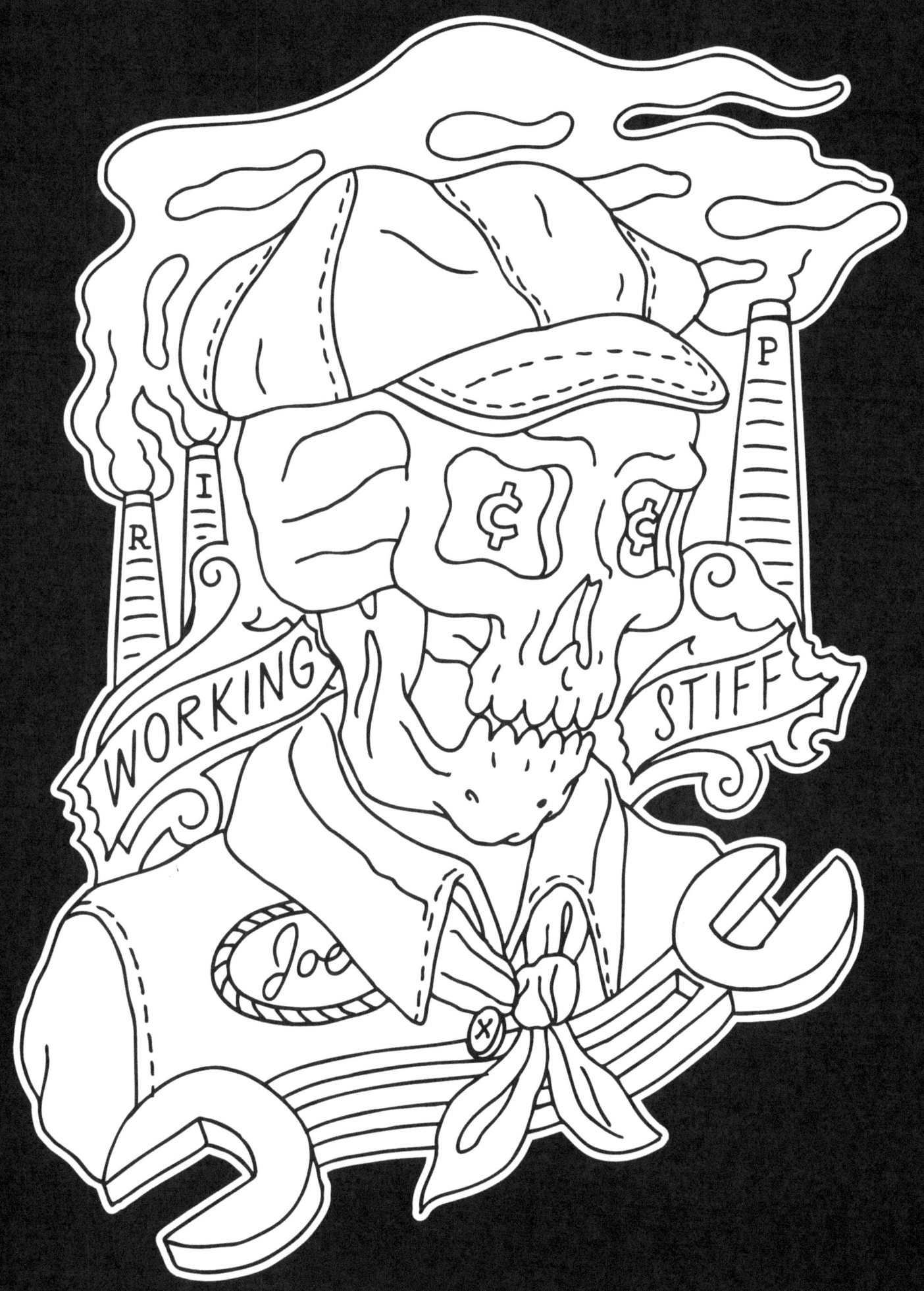

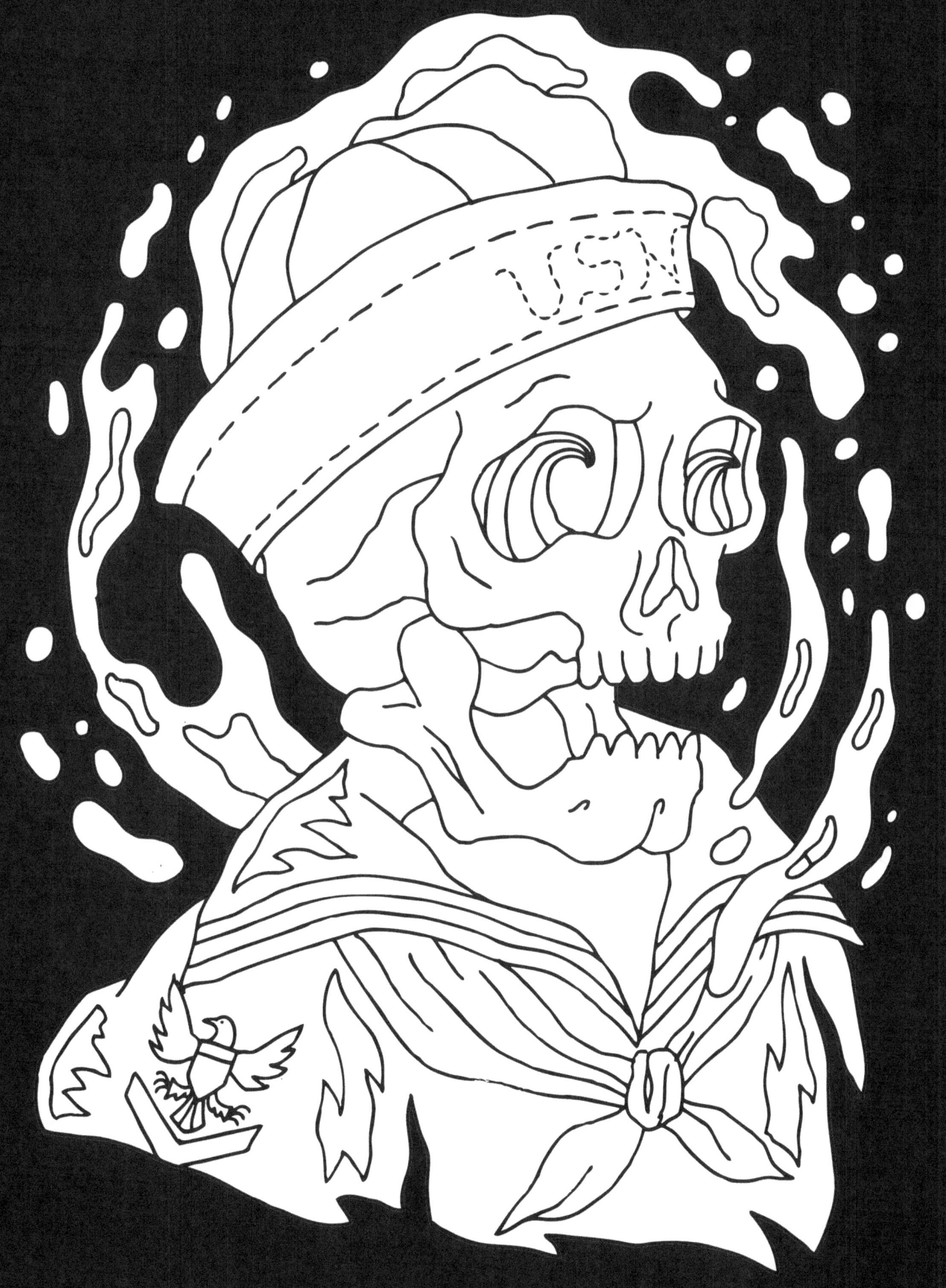

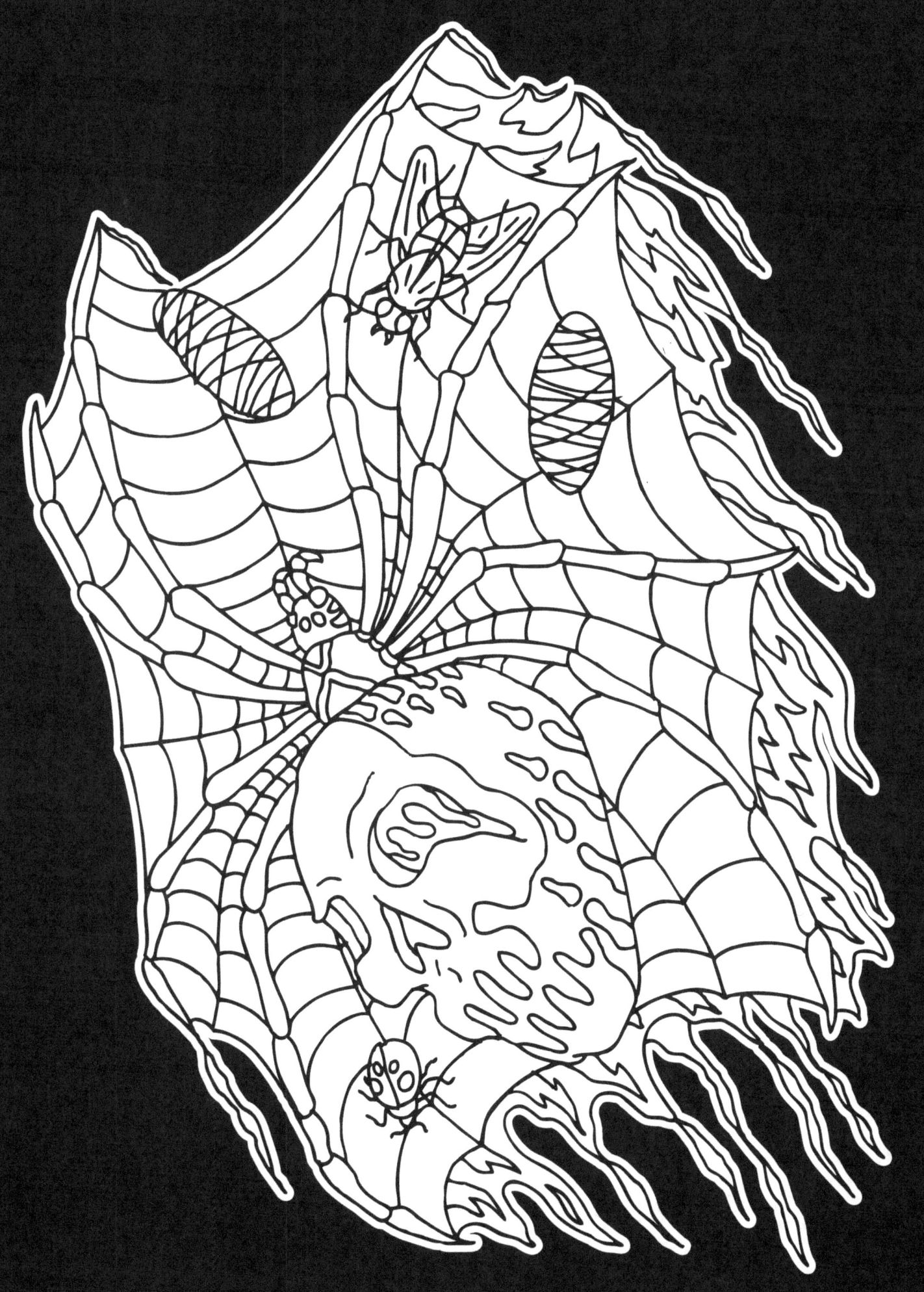

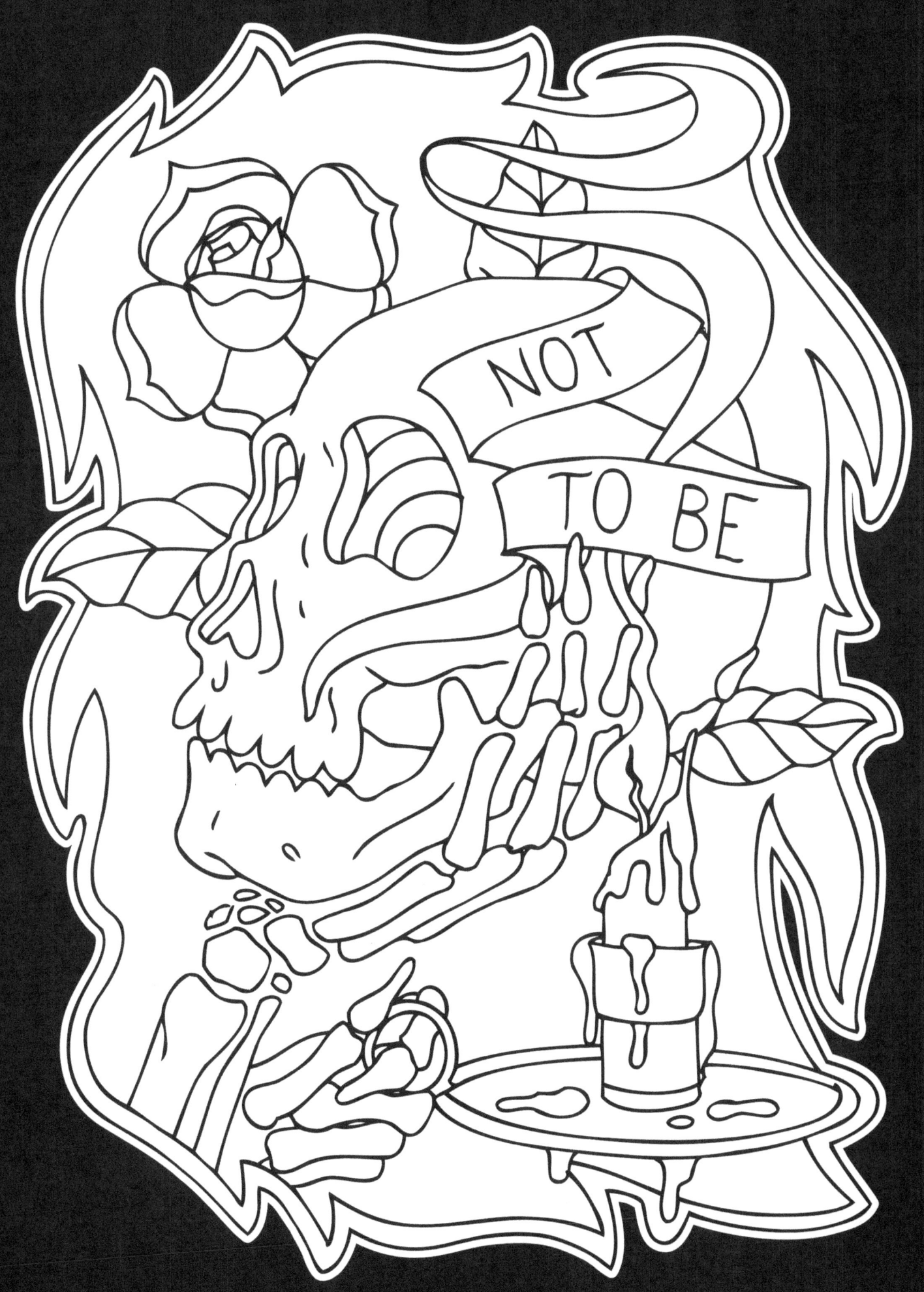

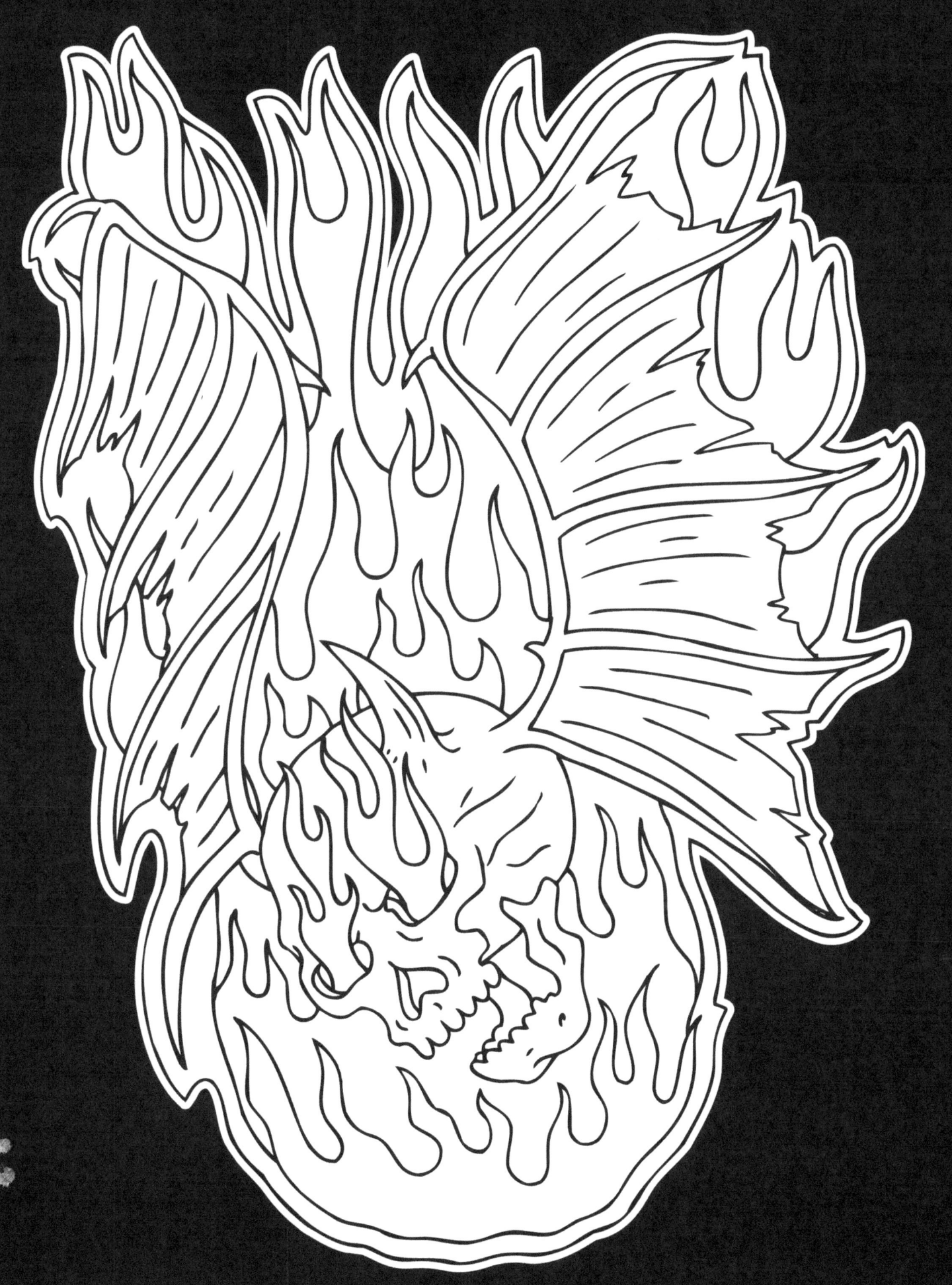

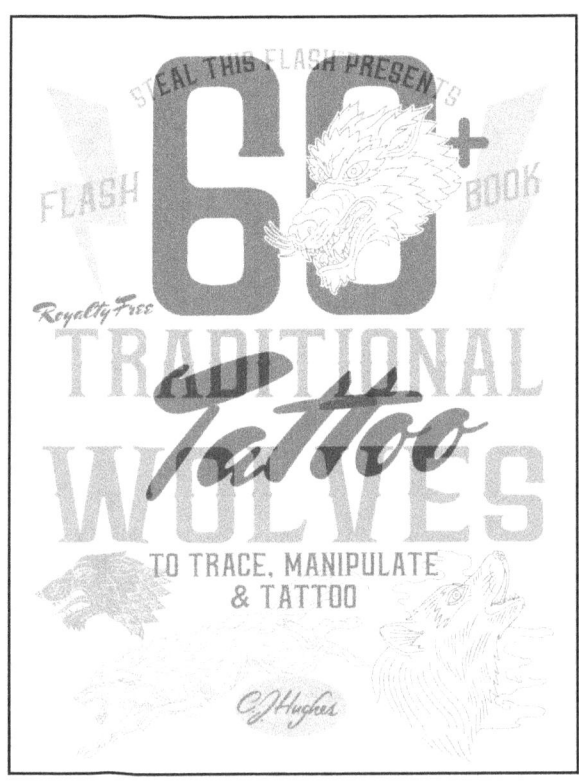
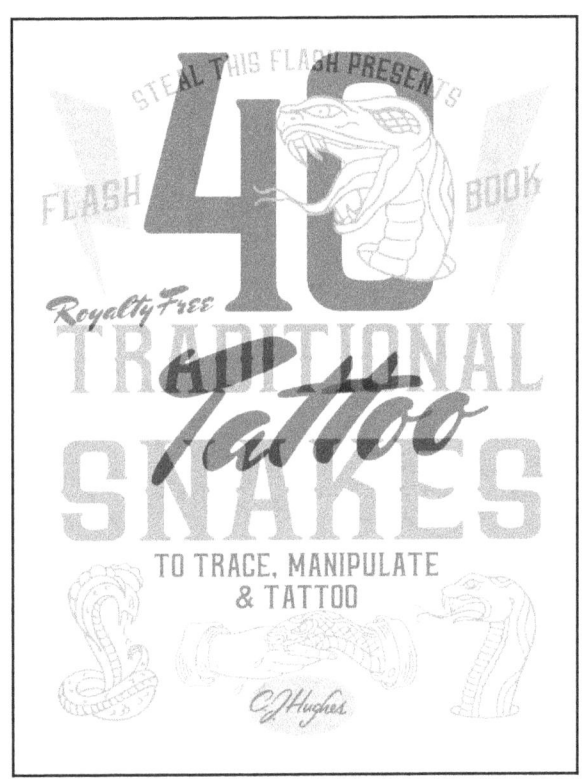
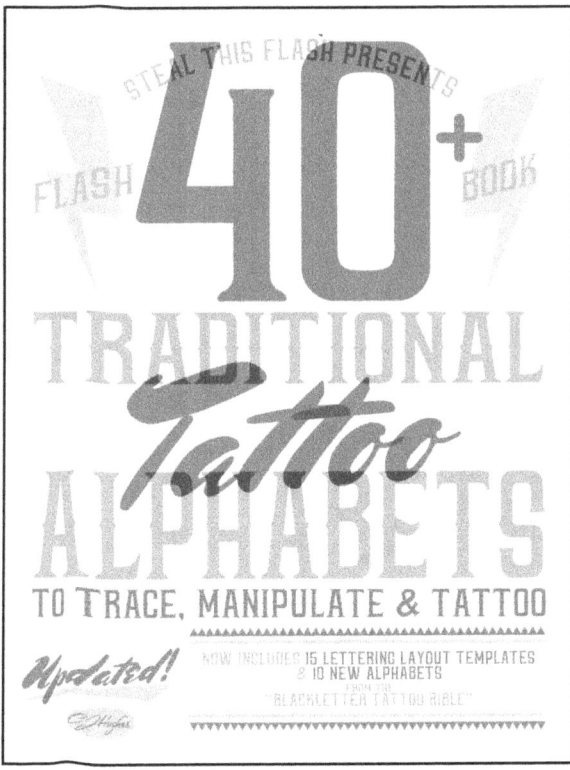
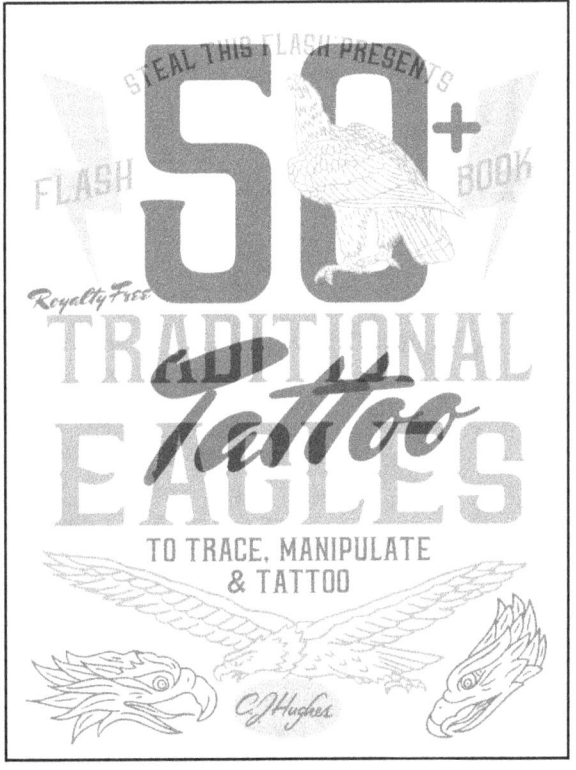

SEARCH "STEAL THIS FLASH" ON AMAZON.COM FOR OUR COMPLETE LINE OF BOOKS.